Creating Your Career Portfolio

At a Glance Guide
2nd Edition

Anna Graf Williams Ph.D.
Karen J. Hall

Prentice Hall
Upper Saddle River, NJ 07458

Library of Congress Cataloging-in-Publication Data

Williams, Anna Graf.
  Creating your career portfolio: at a glance guide / Anna Graf Williams, Karen J. Hall --
2nd ed.
    p. cm.
  Includes index.
  ISBN 0-13-092300-1
  1. Hospitality industry--Vocational guidance. I. Hall, Karen J. II. Title
  TX9I1.3.V62 W53 2001
  647.94'023--dc21

                                                                        00-051675

Executive Editor: Vernon R. Anthony
Production Editor: Barbara Marttine Cappuccio
**Director of Production
  and Manufacturing:** Bruce Johnson
Managing Editor: Mary Carnis
Manufacturing Manager: Ed O'Dougherty
Art Director: Marianne Frasco
Cover Design Coordinator: Miguel Ortiz
Cover Design: Joe Sengotta
Cover Art: Lyn Boyer-Nelles / SIS/Images.com
Marketing Manager: Ryan DeGrote
Editorial Assistant: Susan Kegler
Composition: Karen J. Hall
Printing and Binding: R. R. Donnelley & Sons

Prentice-Hall International (UK) Limited, *London*
Prentice-Hall of Australia Pty. Limited, *Sydney*
Prentice-Hall Canada Inc., *Toronto*
Prentice-Hall Hispanoamericana, S.A., *Mexico*
Prentice-Hall of India Private Limited, *New Delhi*
Prentice-Hall of Japan, Inc., *Tokyo*
Prentice-Hall Singapore Pte. Ltd.
Editora Prentice-Hall do Brasil, Ltda., *Rio de Janeiro*

Prentice
Hall

10 9 8 7 6 5 4 3 2 1
ISBN 0-13-092300-1

Dedication

To everyone who is looking to package who they **really** are... may you find hope and professional success in pursuit of the portfolio process.

CONTENTS

CHAPTER 2—Planning Your Portfolio   21

CHAPTER 3—The Résumé: An Overview of Your Portfolio   35

CHAPTER 4—Proving Your Skills   51

CHAPTER 8—Using Your Portfolio 117

CHAPTER 9—A Matter of Style 129

CHAPTER 1—Resource Guide 147

INDEX—155

Preface (Read This First!)

The question you're probably asking right now is—**what is a career portfolio?** The career portfolio is a tool you use to organize information about yourself, which is then used to help you get a new job or improve your current position. The portfolio is a zippered, 3-ring binder containing information about your beliefs, experiences, and education. It will contain samples of your work, either developed on the job or completed in a classroom setting. The portfolio may also include lists of skills and competencies you possess.

The portfolio is designed by you to help you present the best of yourself to other people. As a tool in an interview or job review, it can be used to generate conversation about your abilities and interests, demonstrate things you've accomplished, and, more important, provide proof of the things you've done. It can distinguish you from the competition and give you an edge. People tend to believe what they can see.

The portfolio can be a powerful tool, but much of its power comes from the process behind it. The process of developing your career portfolio doesn't happen over night. It takes time to accumulate work samples. It takes time to verbalize your beliefs and determine your short- and long-term goals. It is a process of seeing what is good in yourself and incorporating this into the portfolio—documenting awards received, memberships obtained, or your involvement in community service. The process of developing the portfolio helps you become better organized and can give you a greater sense of confidence in yourself because you have **proof** of your own abilities.

Your career portfolio is a tool for life. As your career grows, your portfolio changes and grows with it. New jobs are added to your résumé; new skills are refined and demonstrated. Your file of work samples will continue to grow and expand, and your goals and management philosophy may shift and evolve to higher levels. Your portfolio is an extension of yourself, and you decide what you will make of it.

The **Creating Your Career Portfolio—At a Glance Guide** gives you guidelines for creating your career portfolio. In this book you'll find:

- **a list of supplies you need to begin**
- **general guidelines for organizing your portfolio**
- **detailed discussions of information to be included in different sections**
- **pointers on using the portfolio in an interview or job review**
- **a style guide—containing tips for creating better looking text, photographs, and videos, as well as other ideas for making the production side of the portfolio process run smoothly**

Organization

This book is divided into six sections:

Overview

> **Chapter 1: The Portfolio Process**—An overview of the whole process of portfolio development.

Planning and Collecting Materials

> **Chapter 2: Planning Your Portfolio**—Tools to help you develop your work philosophy and career goals.
> **Chapter 3: The Résumé: An Overview of Your Portfolio**— A look at different types of résumés, both paper and electronic.
> **Chapter 4: Proving Your Skills**— How to collect, select, and assemble your work samples and community service items.
> **Chapter 5: Your Commitment to Personal Growth**—Using the portfolio to track memberships, certifications, and the achievement of your goals.

Putting the Portfolio Together

Chapter 6: The Assembly—Putting it all together; producing the portfolio.

Chapter 7: The Electronic Portfolio—Creating a digital version of your portfolio for the Internet or distribution on CD.

How to Use the Completed Portfolio

Chapter 8: Using Your Portfolio—"Now that I have it, what do I do with it?" Using the portfolio in an interview or to get an internship or co-op experience.

Making the Portfolio Look Good

Chapter 9: A Matter of Style—Production tips focusing on making your documents, pictures, and videos look their best.

Quick Reference Materials

Chapter 10: Resource Guide—Additional resources to make your career portfolio a success, including:
- Supply list with product numbers
- Emergency assembly instructions
- List of action verbs for use in résumés
- Portfolio samples
- Listing of templates included on diskette

We've tried to make this At a Glance Guide live up to its name. If you like to read books straight through from the beginning, you'll find this book organized in a logical way. If you don't like to read a guide until you need help with a particular step, you're in luck. You don't have to read this book from cover to cover to find helpful information. You'll find an overview to the process in this chapter. Along the way you'll see bright ideas, samples, "Ask the Expert" questions, and stories to help you make the most of the career portfolio process.

- When you are ready to work on a particular portion of the portfolio, look up the specific section in Chapters 2-5 for more information.

- For assistance on developing good looking work samples and documents, refer to Chapter 9—A Matter of Style.

- When you're ready to put your portfolio together, turn to Chapter 6, The Assembly, or Chapter 7—The Electronic Portfolio.

- Before you go to your interview or job review, re-read Chapter 8, Using Your Portfolio.

Regardless of how you use this book, you'll find it filled with examples, tips, and ideas that will make the portfolio process truly rewarding.

2nd Edition Highlights

In this 2nd edition, we've added graphics, photos, supply lists, checklists, and many examples given to us by people who have gone through the process of creating their portfolios. We've taken your suggestions, comments, and concerns and integrated them into the process.

We've expanded the section on résumés, talking about résumé styles, what to include and how electronic résumés and portfolios fit. We have expanded our discussions of work samples and details on the contents, and have included suggestions for tracking training and certifications you would like to receive. We've found through our seminars and workshops that people don't always know what they want to do or what their goals are, so we've added career development aids to help you in creating goals and work philsophies.

While seeking career advice about what to do, a very wise person once said,"Concentrate on doing your best—the money will follow." Use the portfolio process to show your best. Often, you have distinct and effective skills hidden in employment and non-employment areas. *Creating Your Career Portfolio* is designed to assist you in pulling together your many skills and competencies. It is the combination of these skills that make you uniquely you.

We hope that you gain insight into yourself, your career interests, and today's job marketplace.

For more hints, stories, seminar information, questions and additional resources for the career portfolio, please check out our website at **http://learnovation.com** If you have any questions or we can be of assistance, please feel free to contact us via mail or e-mail.

Anna Graf Williams, Ph.D., & Karen J. Hall
Learnovation® LLC
10831 Thistle Ridge
Fishers, IN 46038-2254
317-577-1190 / Fax: 317-598-0816
E-mail: **portfolio@learnovation.com**

It's never too late to do what you really want to do. We wish you success in creating your portfolio and growing your career!

1 The Portfolio Process

Five or ten years ago, if you were carrying a portfolio to an interview, you were probably an artist. These people carried around samples of their work in big, bulky folios. To the artist, his or her work and the skill behind it, the style and talents, were on display in the contents of the portfolio. To know the contents of his or her portfolio was to know the artist, the person behind the art.

Employers Want Proof

Today, in the extremely competitive job market of the new millennium, with many highly qualified people competing for the same jobs, employers are looking for new ways to distinguish the excellent people from the average. Having a degree is no longer considered proof of your knowledge, skills, and abilities. Employers are beginning to ask to see results; they want to see physical evidence that shows you possess the abilities you claim. Individuals are also trying to find new ways to distinguish themselves from the rest of the competitors, to find an edge. The career portfolio is designed to do just that: to provide proof of your abilities and produce a tool that is distinctly you.

The portfolio you create through this process will show the best of your work, your accomplishments, and your skills to eager employers. As the artist's portfolio showed the person behind the art, so will your portfolio show the person behind the work samples. The portfolio also includes other support material including lists of documented skills you possess, awards and achievements you've earned, letters of recommendation you've received, your goals for your future, and your vision and beliefs for the future of your industry.

Once you find "the" job, it doesn't mean that your portfolio should be thrown into the dark recesses of your closet, only to be resurrected when you want to begin looking for another position. The portfolio is designed to transition with you into your job. As you continue to collect work samples and proof of your experiences on the job, you can turn your portfolio into a useful tool during a job evaluation or promotion review. Think of the impact you will have when you enter a review, fully prepared to show proof of your accomplishments over the last period!

In this chapter, we will provide you with all the basic information you need to create a career portfolio as we answer these questions:

Why do I need a portfolio?

What's in a portfolio?

What supplies do I need to get started?

How do I put it together?

How will I use this in the job search process?

How can I use this in a job review?

Step 1: Make a Career Plan

Step 2: Gather Work Samples, Certificates, Letters, Projects, Photos, Etc...

Step 3: Update Resume & References; Create Support Materials

Step 4: Purchase Supplies & Assemble the Portfolio

Step 5: Use It in an Interview or Review

The Career Portfolio Process

Why Do I Need a Portfolio?

It's Proof

In an interview or review setting, a career portfolio provides proof of your skills and abilities. Instead of just talking about what you can do during an interview or job review, you can show the person your portfolio—filled with work samples you've created, lists of skills you possess, letters of recommendation, and your professional goals.

An Edge

Recruiters and managers are still not used to seeing portfolios every day. While your portfolio contains samples of your work, it also contains important information about you as a person. You can start interesting conversations that wouldn't be possible without a portfolio in hand. In some cases, having a portfolio can make it easier to stress your strengths in different areas.

It's a Process

The most important thing to remember about portfolio development is that it's a **process**. Of course, the physical portfolio is important, but **the time and effort you put into its development is the true investment in your career**.

Assembling and organizing samples of your work, developing your management philosophy and career goals, and determining the skills and competencies you want to emphasize or obtain in a job situation, are key to the production of the portfolio. You can use the portfolio to track the skills you have and the ones you want to possess. As you work through these areas, you begin to examine your experiences and education from different viewpoints. You learn to recognize your strengths, and find ways to emphasize these through the portfolio. You also are faced with your weaknesses, and, in the process, you find ways to compensate. This process of examining yourself while developing the portfolio can build your confidence, so that there is little, or nothing, that an interviewer or recruiter can ask you that you haven't already thought about.

A Disclaimer

Keep in mind... we don't claim that having a career portfolio is the ultimate answer to your job search. Jobs aren't going to fall out of the sky at your feet if you just raise your portfolio above your head. Developing a portfolio will help you get organized and prepared for the job market. During this process you will be examining your wants, your skills, your abilities, your strengths, and your weaknesses. This should help you feel more confident in your ability to successfully negotiate an interview. Having a neat, well-organized portfolio also projects a professional image back onto you.

While many of the examples in this book take an interviewing approach to portfolio use, don't forget that the portfolio can be a critical tool in job performance reviews and internal job-shifting.

What Is a Portfolio?

By this time, you may be telling yourself that it sounds like there's a lot of work involved in this portfolio process. "Analyzing yourself, collecting samples, writing goals..., can't I just hire someone to do all this work for me?"

The Standard Job Search Tools

First, stop and think about the materials the "average" person creates to get ready for the job search process:

- **Résumé**
- **List of references**
- **Cover letter**

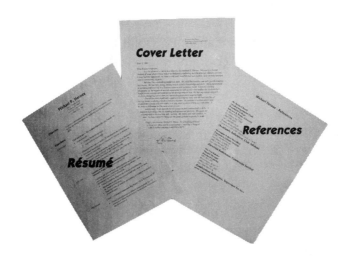

The "average" interview accessories - cover letter, résumé and references

All too often, these are the only materials that people prepare and take with them to an interview. We are taught to believe that our résumé is the key component of the interview process. Write a good cover letter that explains why you are perfect for this organization, include a nicely formatted résumé that shows education and work experience, include some activities and achievements to trigger their curiosity, and you are done with the process.

Make sure you bring a list of people who will say nice things about you to serve as references and you are ready. Keep in mind that the cover letter, résumé, and references are important tools in the job search process. **The résumé and cover letter are the tools you use to get your foot in the door for an interview.** They summarize your abilities and explain why you are well suited to the position. They aren't as helpful during the actual interview, except as a reference for the interviewer.

The Career Portfolio

Now, the person with a Career Portfolio brings a zippered, 3-ring binder to the interview containing a combination of the following tabbed sections:

- **Statement of Originality** — A paragraph stating that this is your work and asking them to keep it confidential.

- **Work Philosophy** — A brief description of your beliefs about yourself and the industry.

- **Career Goals** — Your professional goals for the next two to five years.

- **Résumé** — A brief summary of your education and experiences

- **Skill Areas** — Tabbed sections containing information on your skills and experiences related to a specific area such as Management, Marketing, Training, Technology, Communications, etc.... Each skill area may contain

  ### Work Samples
  Physical examples of your work. Projects, reports, documents, menus, etc. Work samples are proof of your competency in this Skill Area.

  ### Letters of Recommendation
  Letters of support or reference that verify your abilities in this skill area.

  ### Skill Sets
  Checklists of critical skills related to this area. As you attain different levels of competency with each skill, an instructor or employer can sign off on your ability to perform the skill. These are usually pre-existing checklists of skills standardized by an organization.

- **Works in Progress** — A brief list of work, activities, projects, or efforts you are in the process of completing.

- **Certifications, Diplomas, Degrees, or Awards** — Copies of certifications, diplomas, and degrees earned. Copies of special awards and recognitions you have received. Include documentation used to track skills attained for certification.

- **Community Service** — Work samples, letters of recognition, photos of projects completed, programs and brochures relating to community service projects.

- **Professional Memberships and Certifications** — Membership cards, citations, and letters related to professional organizations.

- **Academic Plan of Study** — A copy of your plan of study that lists courses you have taken to fulfill your degree.

- **Faculty and Employer Biographies** — Brief descriptions of the people whose names appear throughout the portfolio—who they are and what they do.

- **References** — A list of people who can verify your character, academic record, or employment history.

The Career Portfolio

Now, which person do you think looks more prepared for the interview - the one with the average tools or the career portfolio?

What Supplies Do I Need to Get Started?

The materials you use to create the portfolio serve two purposes:

1. To help organize your materials and documents so you can easily customize your portfolio for a given interview or review period; and

2. To make your portfolio look professional. A quick shopping list of supplies, including brands and product numbers, is found in Chapter 10, Resource Guide.

Portfolio Supplies

Purchase These Supplies

Here is a list of supplies that will help you begin the process of collecting and assembling your portfolio:

- **Plastic file tote box** —(1 to 2 boxes) Used to store work samples, materials, etc.. Should be able to hold hanging file folders.
- **Hanging file folders**—20 to 30 folders.

- **Zippered, 3-ring notebook**—Cloth, leather, or vinyl with 1-1/2" to 2" rings. Cloth is the cheapest, ranging from $7-$20. Vinyl costs $20-$30, and leather binders often run from $60 or more. All are available at local office supply stores.

- **Sheet protectors**—Clear, plastic, 3-hole punched pockets that hold documents and work samples. They protect your portfolio and give it a professional look. Avoid the non-glare variety because they are harder to read.

- **Connected sheet protectors**—Three to five sets of sheet protectors, bound together in sets of 5 or 10 sheets. These are great for keeping projects and work samples neatly together in your file box. This makes it easier to swap work samples in and out of the portfolio.

- **Extra-wide 3-ring tabs with labels**—Page protectors are wider than ordinary 3-ring tabs. You need to find extra-wide tabs made for use with page protectors.

- **Paper**—Use a high quality paper. See Chapter 9, A Matter of Style, for suggestions on paper choices.

- **Business cards**—Blank sheets of cards are used to create work sample overview cards for work samples. You don't have to use plain white cards—select something that shows your style.

- **Photo sheet holders**—Plastic sheets that can hold vertical and/or horizontal pictures.

- **Name plate or vinyl card holder**—Used on the cover of the portfolio to identify it as your property.

- **Zippered pouch**—(optional) Holds videos.

- **Diskette holders**—(optional) Holds project diskettes.

A more detailed list, including brands and product numbers, can be found in Chapter 10, Resource Guide.

Have Access to This Equipment

A professional portfolio looks good and feels good. To make this portfolio something you can be proud of, you should plan on using the following equipment when you create documents and work samples to enhance the quality of your career portfolio:

- **Computer**—You should have access to current versions of word processor, graphic presentation, and spreadsheet packages.
- **Printer**— Laser or high-quality ink jet.
- **Color flatbed scanner** —Used to scan certificates, work samples, etc.
- **Color copier or color printer** —Used to reproduce work samples, certificates, awards, etc.
- **Film Camera or Digital Camera**—Used for photographing work samples and documenting other activities.
- **Video camera** —Videotape yourself in action when necessary.

Things You Don't Need

- **Ink pens**—Do everything on a computer.
- **3-hole paper punch**—Use page protectors instead of punching holes. Your work will look more professional.
- **Paper clips, staples, and tape**—If you want to connect several pages or display a work sample, use a set of connected sheet protectors.

Creating and Using the Portfolio

A Little Planning Goes a Long Way

Getting the supplies together to produce your portfolio is the easy part. Deciding what to put into your portfolio requires planning and organization. Begin by analyzing your strengths and weaknesses. What are you best at? Which skills and abilities do you want to emphasize? Are there things that you'd rather not have people ask about, or skills that you know you are lacking but would like to have? Taking the time to examine your experiences and abilities will help you focus on your key skill areas that you will

Bright Idea!

Save everything you create! You can decide which samples to use later when you're ready to assemble your portfolio.

use in your portfolio. You will also use the planning time to write your work philosophy and career goals. A **work philosophy** gives an employer a unique perspective on you as a person through your personal beliefs about work and your industry. Career **goals** show the employer that you have a plan for your life.

Collect and Organize Work Samples

Once you have decided on your key skill areas, you need to find things that demonstrate your abilities in each area. You can use projects, reports, photos, letters of recommendation, certificates, newspaper articles, and any materials you have created on the job, in school, or during community service.

Putting the Portfolio Together

When you are ready to assemble your portfolio, you will gather your supplies together, along with a good friend (this is very important!!), and choose the samples to use.

- Decide what key skill areas you want to focus on, and create a **tab page** for each. Then pick three or four of your best samples for each area and put them into sheet protectors or photo holders.

- Create **work sample overview cards** for each sample to help a viewer quickly identify the type of sample and what it represents. The card is slid into the sheet protector and floats over the top of the sample.

- Create a **statement of originality and confidentiality** to indicate that this is your work.
- Print out your **work philosophy** and **career goals**, your **résumé** and **references**.
- Create a list of **works in progress** to indicate projects you are working on now for which you have no work samples.
- Create a list of your professional **memberships** and create a **Faculty and Employer Bio Sheet** listing information about the people mentioned in your portfolio.
- Put copies of your **certificates** and **awards** in sheet protectors, along with an **academic plan of study** if you want to stress your coursework.
- Set up and print out the **tabs** and insert them in the dividers.

As you are assembling your portfolio, be sure to reference the Style Guide in Chapter 9 for tips on making your portfolio look its best. Once you put your portfolio together, you're ready to put it to good use.

Using the Portfolio in the Job Search Process

So, how do you put the portfolio to work? Remember that it's your résumé that helps get you the interview. Once you have an interview scheduled, you'll want to make sure that the samples in your portfolio show you to the best advantage. Each employer is looking for different things, and you may need to use different work samples to prove different skills. Customize your portfolio for the interview.

During the interview you can use your portfolio to answer questions or show examples of your work. Just by having a portfolio along, you can show the interviewer that you have organization skills and are focused on your career. Your portfolio can make a lasting impression. Some people have also sent copies of their portfolio along with the thank you letter after an interview to reinforce their skills, especially when they didn't have a chance to fully use their portfolio during the interview itself.

How Will I Use This in a Job Review?

If you already have a job and you want to shine in a performance review, or want to have an edge in the promotion process, you can use your portfolio to keep track of what you have accomplished and present it in an organized manner.

James' Story

James was feeling a little down after his interview. The interviewer hadn't seemed too interested in his portfolio and he had really wanted to show him some of the things he had created on the job. James went to the copy shop and made a spiral-bound color copy of his portfolio. He sent the copy to the interviewer with his thank you letter. In the letter he asked the interviewer to take a few minutes and glance at the portfolio, being sure to point out some of the highlights.

James' extra effort made the difference. The interviewer did take the time to look through his portfolio and was impressed by what he saw. James was called back for a second interview and got the job and a larger starting salary based on the contents of his career portfolio.

Steps for Growing Your Career

You can use your portfolio on the job to keep track of what you have done and what you plan to do in the next quarter. Here are some ideas of things to record:

- Keep a listing of projects and documents you have completed during the last review period.

- Keep track of the committees and projects you've worked with.

- Set goals for each review period and track your achievements. Show how your goals help meet the goals of the company.
- Include any community service activities in which you have been involved.
- If necessary, update your work philosophy and your career goals, both outside and within the company.
- Keep copies of thank you letters and memos that document teamwork or cooperation.
- If your supervisor is new, you should include highlights of your career since you were hired by the company.
- Let your supervisor know well in advance of your review that you are using a career portfolio.

Before Your Review

Talk with your boss and explain the contents of your portfolio. Drop off the portfolio a few days before your review so he or she has time to review it. Then discuss it at your annual review.

Kathy's Job Review

Kathy's boss was a little intimidated by her portfolio. When she saw the updated résumé and references, she was sure she was ready to look for a job. Kathy assured her that her portfolio was a "career" portfolio, tracking her performance and abilities on the job. Keeping it up to date showed her organization skills and helped her track her goals and achievements.

How Will I Use This in an Internal Job Shift?

The portfolio can be a great help if you are looking to advance within a company, or to shift laterally in the company. People job shift inside a company in order to change their responsibilities, find new growth opportunities, or obtain salary increases. An up-to-date portfolio can help you to position yourself where you want to be.

Your portfolio needs to contain samples of your accomplishments in your department. You should also include samples that show your management skills, of people or projects. Make sure you note any committees or special projects you have been involved in, and highlight your product knowledge and transferable skills.

Transferable Skills and Job Shifting

George was a technical writer in the company, writing documentation and manuals for a software program. When a position opened up in the Training Development area of the company to create training for the same programs, he applied. In his portfolio, he highlighted his current experience with the company, his extensive product knowledge and writing ability. He used his portfolio to document his training experience and educational background in training and emphasized skills that he could use in both positions.

Using the Portfolio to Keep Track of Certifications & Professional Development

A portfolio is a great tool for managing information. More organizations are beginning to use portfolios to keep track of member progress toward industry certification. Many people use a portfolio only for tracking things they've accomplished; others use it as a means of assessment, where the contents of the portfolio indicate the success of the program.

The portfolio can be a tool for tracking your progress toward specific certification in your field. Whether you are working to become a certified CPA, Novell administrator, or Registered Dietician, you can use the career portfolio as a place to track your progress toward your goal. Depending on your certification process, you may have a structured set of materials that you can put into the portfolio where you can list or mark down what you have accomplished to date. If no formal plan fits, you can create your own forms and lists to track your progress.

Remember, the portfolio isn't just for getting a new job; it's a tool for tracking your skills and abilities. As you obtain new skills, you should add them to the portfolio. Keep this document up to date, and you'll be ready for anything.

Sounds Great—But It Won't Work for Me

"Sounds great but it won't work for me." If there is something in your gut that makes you uneasy with the prospect of developing a portfolio, there are two possible explanations. First, you may be a master procrastinator and this is your normal response to work efforts. The second, and more likely possibility, is that you can't see yourself with enough work samples to make the portfolio process work.

Common Stumbling Blocks:

- **Lack of physical work samples.**
- **Unclear personal goals.**
- **Not sure how to use the portfolio in your particular industry or profession.**

Throughout the development of this portfolio process, several people kept telling us— "this sounds great but.." We kept trying to figure out the reasons for their resistance to the process. Was it too much work? Were they unsure about how to actually use it in an interview? Finally, after observing one person's struggle during a full-time job search, we discovered the problem.

The Portfolio in Action

Our friend George wanted a different job and had background and experience to do many different kinds of work. George had a solid, formal education and lots of community service background, but he kept blocking when we offered to help him put together the portfolio. This went on for months. Then all of a sudden, one employer said, "Could you do a presentation for us and bring us some of your work to the interview tomorrow?" We followed the guidelines for the "Emergency Portfolio" in Chapter 10, Resource Guide, and helped him create a portfolio for the next day. He admitted that "A portfolio was the best way to organize my work."

George found that the process wasn't so bad, and the portfolio worked well in the interview. When we quizzed him about what kept him from doing it earlier, he said, "Most of the résumés I sent out were for jobs where I didn't have an exact match to the company." He felt that the portfolio worked best when you could match your work samples to the skills needed by the company.

The story continues. In subsequent interviews he used his portfolio each time. George said, "Most people conducting the interview don't know how to get information out of you. This portfolio stuff works because you can prompt the interviewer to ask better questions." In several interviews, George found that the interviewer wasn't very interested in the portfolio at the beginning of the interview, but when he used it to answer a question about his experience, it peaked the interviewer's curiosity enough to look through the whole portfolio. Every time he was asked how well the portfolio worked, he would say, "It blew them away—they were impressed."

We're happy to say George found a job where his talents and experiences could be well used. "I might have still gotten this job without it," he said, "but the portfolio made the interview go more smoothly. The interviewers were impressed by the portfolio, and it made me a more visible candidate. At my 90-day review I learned that I had started about $5,000 higher than average because I had the portfolio and could show them my skills." The moral of the story is... if you are feeling overwhelmed and uneasy about the portfolio, be sure you are seeking out positions that are really you.

Sounds Great—But I Don't Need It, I Have Lots of Job Offers

"The job market is real good right now and I have lots of offers." If this sounds like you—Congratulations! It would be easy to take the path of least resistance here. Consider however, that using the portfolio may help to "up the offer." Remember that getting the job is the first hurdle, keeping it is the next, followed by the goal of getting promoted and rewarded for the job.

Upping the Offer

When you have a portfolio, you have your professional goals spelled out. You can use this section, along with your work samples, to get more money or better benefits. Pam developed her portfolio, after receiving three offers, to help justify her negotiations for benefits and perks. The money being offered may be preset, but the benefits package can often be expanded for secondary benefits. Secondary benefits are the non-insurance and retirement benefits. She used her portfolio to demonstrate her abilities and her need for professional development. Each of these companies agreed to pay for her professional memberships and one three-day professional meeting. This would save her an average of $1,200 out-of-pocket expenses per year. She was also able to convince her eventual employer to purchase an additional copy of the software they used in the office for home use. This made her job easier by having the same software at home to do her work.

There is something about the portfolio process which causes you to reflect on who you are, what you want to do, and to search out what you are good at doing. Let's focus on getting you rewarded for your work. Using the portfolio process for upping the offer in the interview sets you up to use it on the job during your performance appraisals or year-end reviews.

I Need a Portfolio Now!!!

"Oh, it won't take that long to put it together."

"I have one that I used last time."

"My interview is tomorrow and I have to do all this before I can start on my portfolio?"

"Help, I have an interview tomorrow and they asked me to bring work samples!"

If you've just purchased this book and want to put together a portfolio for an interview tomorrow morning, or if you've had this book for a while and suddenly your interview is upon you, there's still hope. Based on several frantic experiences of our own, rest assured you can put together a basic career portfolio in three hours if you have a computer, printer, and your best friend's help. See Chapter 10, Resource Guide, on page 148 for all the details on creating the emergency portfolio.

Read On

You now have the basic ideas necessary to create your portfolio. In the following chapters you will learn how to plan and organize your portfolio and make a personalized tool for career success.

We've organized these sections as you would position them in the completed portfolio. This doesn't mean you will be developing your materials in this order; quite the contrary, you have to make the most of the opportunities at hand. You'll probably be saving projects and papers or securing signatures for skill areas long before you focus your résumé. Refer to Chapter 6, Assembly, for tips on organizing and creating the actual portfolio.

Keep in mind as you continue through this guide that the portfolio provides:

Insight into you as a person

- Statement of Originality & Confidentiality

- Work Philosophy
- Goals

A summary of your portfolio

- Résumé

Proof of your abilities

- Skill Areas containing:
    - Work Samples
    - Letters of Recommendation
    - Skill Sets
    - Community Service
    - Certifications, Awards, Degrees, and Diplomas
    - Works in Progress

Your commitment to your own personal and professional growth

- Professional Memberships
- Professional Development Plans

Reference materials

- Academic Plan of Study
- Faculty and Employer Bios
- References

2 PLANNING YOUR PORTFOLIO

If you could have anything in your life, what would you want? This is the place where you begin to evaluate your work philosophy and establish goals. This chapter will provide you with the mechanics and several tools for generating the pieces you need in your portfolio. You analyze current and yet to be acquired skills. This is where you design your career. Keep in mind that your career is more than a job—it's the paths those jobs take.

This is a process you do when you are looking for a job, and where you should go three to four months into the job to connect with the corporate culture and company goals.

Designing Your Career

You've got to have a goal. If you don't, your career will be one reaction after another. With a plan in place from your master design you're able to maintain your focus. You may encounter opportunities or careers shifts or additional training. With your career goals in mind, you can determine which opportunities to accept and which to decline. This is the part of the process where you get a master plan. Be sure you hold a higher vision of your potential when you do it.

Work Philosophy

A work philosophy is a statement of your beliefs about yourself, people, and your outlook on life in your industry. Your work philosophy is often used by an interviewer to see if you match a company's corporate culture. After reading this statement, a potential employer should know whether you would fit the "style" of the organization.

Make sure you have a friend to assist you when you're ready to develop your work philosophy. Your friend can help you to take your beliefs and the ideas that you have internalized and verbalize it on to paper. Many people know in their hearts what they believe, but they've never put it into words. Your work philosophy might also be called a management philosophy.

What you need to know about your philosophy...

- **Think about it** — Don't expect to "whip out" a work philosophy or personal mission statement in 10 or 20 minutes. It usually takes a few days worth of thought and reflection before the "final draft" is ready.

- **Place your most important belief first** —Your work philosophy should be unique to you, communicate who you are and what makes you different from others who may want the same position.

- **Length** — Your work philosophy should be one to four sentences in length, and should address your beliefs and your outlook on people.

- **Use bullets** —Consider using bullet points for added clarity.

- **Have a friend review it for clarity** —After you have it on paper, ask a few friends to read it for clarity—not approval. Remember that your work philosophy is never right or wrong; it represents your key beliefs and values.

Here's the work philosophy of one graduating student:

Work Philosophy

- The customer always comes first.
- Financial and operational controls must be clear to all members of the company.
- Technology will be critical in reaching the guests and communicating within the company.
- I want to be part of a winning team.

 Template

Use the **Work Philosophy and Goals.doc** file on the companion diskette as a starting point to developing your own portfolio.

Goals

Your goals set a direction for your career and are general in nature. The goals in your portfolio should focus on the professional achievements, skills, and knowledge you want to acquire over the next several years. Companies use these goals to anticipate your developmental needs and interests. They also show management and recruiters that you do indeed have a plan for your future.

Here again, a friend can help you develop your goals. He or she can ask questions that make you think about your goals and can help make sure your goals make sense.

Making Your Goals Work

- **Plan your goals for two to five years from now** — When writing goals, think ahead several years beyond today. What do you want to be doing in two years? What do you want to have accomplished four years from today? Goals written for one year or less are often too narrow in focus, and usually concentrate on learning a new position rather than planning for the future. You should also make sure your goals are not so specific as to imply only a narrow interest in the industry or in a specific job. If you are starting in an entry-level position, think about the job you want to be doing in two to three years. Goals can help share your vision for where you will fit in the organization in the future.

- **Make your goals measurable** — Your goals should be specific enough that you will know when you've achieved them. We measure goals in terms of time, money, and resources.

   Too broad:
   "To expand my technical knowledge."

   Good:
   "To develop my database skills by attending a class on Microsoft Access by May 2001."

- **Goals are different from career objectives** — Career objectives are broad and set a direction for your career. Goals are more specific; they include shorter-range objectives that are measurable.

- **Write three to five goals** — If you only write one or two goals, you may appear unfocused and give the impression that you're not really interested in advancing your career.

- **Don't make your goals too personal** — Goals such as losing weight, attending a wild orgy, or winning a marathon can alienate your interviewer; it may give the person more information than he/she may want to know about sensitive topics. Keep your goals professional and related to your career.

Here is a sample of goals that are appropriate for individuals just starting their careers:

Two-Year Goals

- To hold a leadership role in my department
- To hold at least one active professional membership
- To further develop my computer application skills as they apply to controlling costs
- To earn the customer service award
- To apply my creativity to develop new menus

 Template

Use the **Work Philosophy and Goals.doc** file on the companion diskette as a starting point to developing your own goal and your philosophy.

Your Career Plan

OK... by now you have already dealt with your work philosophy and flushed out at least a couple of year's worth of goals. What happens next? You have spent your time on the "big picture"— NOW you need an action plan. Consider what you can gain by doing a thorough analysis of your skills, interests, and abilities from the professional and personal perspective. Let's start with a couple of key tools for analyzing and getting a plan—the SWOT analysis and the storyboard. Successful organizations and individuals use both of these techniques to develop action plans.

Strengths, Weaknesses, Opportunities, and Threats to Your Career (SWOT)

A SWOT analysis is a method of looking at the **S**trengths, **W**eaknesses, **O**pportunities, and **T**hreats in a specific situation. In this case, we are applying the process to your career. Strengths and weaknesses are personal to you, they are things you can control. One person may list good computer skills as a strength yet another person lists it as a weakness to their career. How skilled you are is something you can control because you can choose to focus on those skills or you can decide to take a class to improve your skills.

Opportunities and threats are things in your environment that you can't control. Opportunities are positive things that work to your advantage, whereas threats are negative factors that could be a potential setback to your plans. A person considering medical school might list the high salary and prestige of being a doctor as an opportunity, whereas the cost of medical school and the length of time needed to obtain a degree could be listed as a threat. The salary of a doctor and the cost of medical school are things that you can't control.

The SWOT analysis is the part of the process where you really size up what you have to offer. When doing a SWOT you look at all the characteristics that influence your professional and personal life. Take a look at this shopping list of characteristics for things you **can control** and record your answers on the templates on pages 28 and 29:

- Skills in Your Field
- Supervision/Management/Leadership Abilities
- Types of Teams
- Communication (written, electronic, verbal, and non-verbal)
- Technology (types of software and projects)
- Social (professional and service groups)
- Personal Areas such as Community Service

Give some additional consideration in your analysis to those things you do **not control**:

- Economy/Demand for Jobs
- Social Trends (health, transportation, and e-commerce)
- Political (government or workplace)
- Technology
- Advancement Availability (career path, age and experience of those around you)
- Location (job, geography)
- Workplace Culture (work ethic, family values, and uses of power)
- Required Education (certifications, etc.)

SWOT started as a way to analyze non-profit organizations and has, in the last 30 years, transitioned to business planning as well as personal planning. You can use a SWOT analysis to help explore issues, skills, strengths, and weaknesses you have in your career search. Look at your skills and abilities in your personal and professional life. Where are you now? What are your strengths? What are your weaknesses? List them under the major headings, and then rank them from the strongest to the weakest. Once you know your strengths and weaknesses, you will know what areas to promote and can formulate your goals for where you would like to be.

Look at the factors above and list items that have an impact on your career. Look at the career you want. What education do you need? Can you get a job anywhere, or only in a certain part of the country? Do you want to work in a office environment or are you a person who can't stand the thought of being tied down all day? Is the industry you are aiming for in a growth spurt, or are there too many qualified people now? These are all factors that you can't control but which will influence your career. Rank them from highest impact to lowest. Knowledge of these issues can help you make better decisions.

SWOT Analysis - Your Career

Things You Control

Rank	Your STRENGTHS	Your WEAKNESSES	Rank
	Skills related to your field	Skills related to your field	
	Management	Management	
	Teamwork	Teamwork	
	Communication	Communication	
	Technology - (software, Internet telecommunications, etc.)	Technology - (software, Internet telecommunications, etc.)	
	Social	Social	
	Personal Areas Family/Friends/ Spiritual/Financial/Health	Personal Areas Family/Friends/ Spiritual/Financial/Health	

Look at your skills and abilities in your personal and professional life. Where are you now? What are your strengths? What are your weaknesses? List them under the major headings; then rank them from the strongest to the weakest. Once you know your strengths and weaknesses, you will know what areas to promote and can formulate your goals for where you would like to be.

SWOT Analysis - Your Career

Things You Don't Control

Rank	OPPORTUNITIES you can use	THREATS that face you	Rank
	Economy/Demand for Jobs	Economy/Demand for Jobs	
	Social Trends	Social Trends	
	Political (government or workplace)	Political (government or workplace)	
	Techonology	Techonology	
	Advancement Availability	Advancement Availability	
	Location (Job, Geography)	Location (Job, Geography)	
	Workplace Culture	Workplace Culture	
	Required Education	Required Education	

Look at the factors above and list the items that have an impact on your career. Look at the career you want. What is the education that you need? Can you get a job anywhere in or only in a certain part of the country? Do you want to work in an office environment or can't you stand the thought of being tied down all day? Is the industry you are aiming for in a growth spurt, or are there too many qualified people now? These are all factors that you can't control which will influence your career. Rank them from highest impact to lowest. Knowledge of these issues can help you make better decisions.

Template

The Career SWOT sheets shown on the previous two pages are available on the companion diskette (**SWOT Analysis.doc**).

Ask the Expert - I want to be Management!

Q. Currently I am entering a new position at work as an application systems analyst. However the management position for that group will be vacant by the time I get fully started. I am almost finished with my Graduate degree in Information Systems, and would desperately like a management position to be on track with my career path. In the past it seems management positions always escape me. My question is: What steps should I be taking at this time to hopefully be considered for the position now or in the near future?

A. Frequently in the field of technology applications it is assumed that systems analysts are not management. You need to gather together evidence of your management abilities. Perhaps you have some jobs in your history with some transferable skills or some community service activities which will give evidence of your management abilities. Consider developing a career portfolio and focusing one entire tabbed section to management work samples and letters of support. In your case, letters from peers or superiors who believe you to have management abilities would be helpful. Start your career portfolio off by including your work philosophy with management emphasis; goals with management elements; work samples organized into key areas, community service with transferable skills, works in progress; professional associations where you have taken a leadership role as well as credentials and references. Take time to organize your best work samples into tech areas of emphasis; supervision/management; specialities.

🌱 Ask the Expert - I can do the job, but I can't prove it!

Q. I have worked at the same location for 25+ years, most of these at the same job. I had complete responsibility for ordering, receiving, inventory (and reporting), and warehousing for packaging; also legality, graphics, budgets, and everything. Not a huge company so I was, for the most part, able to handle this on my own. Except for a brief period where I took over for a manager for several months, I had no one reporting to me. I worked myself up to a supervisory pay scale; I had no fancy title. And then here comes reorganization. I lost my life-long position!

Now I'm looking for a warehouse manager (or even supervisor) position. It seems that, for the larger companys anyway, they require 3, 5, or 7 years of supervisory experience; sometimes a BA (I have an AA). I have extensive background in operations but I don't have years of supervisory experience that I can put on a résumé. I personally feel that I can handle managerial duties; I've actually been doing them for years, but I have nothing in black and white that proves it. (My employer is not going to back me up on this; how things change.) How do I handle not ever having a supervisory/management/fancy title?

A. You need to pull together work samples in any way or fashion you can. Be sure to include your community service where you can show transferable skills of supervision and leadership. It seems you have may quality traits to emphasize -- not the least of which is loyalty. Consider taking continuing studies classes from the local university where you could pick up a certificate in management or supervision. In the meantime, be sure that you shop for a corporate culture that will respect your values and quality traits.

Time to Tell Your Story

Storyboarding is that process where you "draw mental pictures" of all aspects of your story. Consider storyboarding as a strategic planning tool. Storyboarding is a way to manage the big picture and develop details. Storyboarding got its start with the great Walt Disney who created the process to lay out the animated movies and to carry multiple storylines. This is where you map out your skills and abilities — your story.

Use storyboarding to help map out your career

How to Storyboard

- Get yourself a large sheet of paper and sticky notes or a big board.

- Write your goal statements across the top of the paper to serve as categories for organizing skills.

- Work through these questions, putting each item answer on a separate sticky note. Concentrate on skills and keywords.

- Post the sticky notes into the goal categories.

- Make a note or map out the work samples you have or need to seek out.

- Take a picture of your map or copy down all your notes and then create your portfolio.

Storyboarding works by allowing you to make multiple lists and to develop and link ideas. A good way is to begin is to answer these questions: What skills are needed in the position I am working to secure or advance in?

- What skills do I have?

- What am I good at?

- How can I use my current skills in my work?

- What projects have I worked on in school or on the job?

- What do my friends or enemies think I'm good at doing?

Building Your Portfolio Plan

Take the results of your SWOT or storyboard process and build your portfolio plan. It is critical to your success to understand what you have as skills and characteristics, and to create a vision for what you want to do in your profession.

Taking time to evaluate your career and focus your goals will help you in the next phase of the portfolio - putting your résumé together and finding and gathering the proof of your abilities. Don't underestimate the importance of the activities in this chapter. Having the focus will help you determine how to build skill sections of your portfolio and help you focus on producing a valuable tool.

3 The Résumé: An Overview of Your Portfolio

Everyone knows about résumés. They are the most common vehicle used in the job-hunting process and are used to convey information about your experiences and qualifications. A résumé usually contains a survey of your education, work experiences, and qualifications for a position. When used in conjunction with your portfolio, the résumé serves as a springboard for introducing your portfolio into the conversation. It is also provides a summary of the contents of the portfolio.

This chapter gives general suggestions for creating your résumé. If you want specific details, you'll find a wealth of information on the Internet. At the end of this chapter we've included some good websites to help guide you in the process of creating your résumé and making it look its best.

What Goes in Your Résumé?

Creating a résumé is often a daunting task for anyone about to pursue a job search. It is the crucial tool needed to get an interview, and creating it can be a painful experience. There is so much conflicting information about résumés available today. "Can it be more than one page?" "Does my education or experience go first?" "What do I do about gaps in my experience?" "How do I make myself look really good without bragging?" "How do I make them see my résumé in the huge pile on the secretary's desk?" "How far back should I go with my experience?" What if I'm switching fields?" "What if I don't have all the qualifications they are looking for?" The questions go on...

Résumé Basics

If you are just entering the workforce, your résumé will look very different from that of a person who has had several years of experience in his or her field. In general, most résumés have a combination of the following sections:

Career Objective/Career Summary- A **career objective** is an overview of the kind of work you want to do: a one-or two- sentence summary of your career goals. If you have been in the workforce for several years, you may want to use a career summary. The **career summary** consists of two to three sentences which briefly outline your career history.

Education - Include any formal education, degrees obtained and in progress, the institution, dates attended, and the focus of your degree(s).

- The less experience you have, the more you need to build up your education. You might consider listing classes you took which are relevant to the field you are entering.
- List any formal education or training programs you have taken which relate to your field.
- List your most recent achievements first.

Work Experience or Skills - Include your job title, name of the organization, dates employed, and an overview of your skills and experience.

- If your work experience is stronger and/or more recent than your education, list your work experience first.
- List your accomplishments and/or responsibilities with each position.
- List your most recent experience first.

Professional Memberships and Services, Awards Received— Include memberships and awards that demonstrate your abilities, enhance your leadership or document your skills.

Community Service - List organizations and your involvement with them.

Contact Information - Your name, address, phone number, fax number, e-mail address.

Let Them Know You Have a Portfolio - Your résumé also needs a line at the bottom of the last page indicating that your portfolio is available for review:

Career Portfolio and References available for review

Organizing Your Résumé

There are several standard ways of organizing a résumé, depending on your experiences, skills, and target industry:

- **Chronological Résumés**—Information is organized by date. Information is listed in order of time elapsed, with the most recent experiences first.This is the most common and straightforward résumé format.

- **Functional Résumés**—This type of résumé is designed to highlight accomplishments and specific skills. It is organized by the different kinds of skills you can perform, such as management skills, marketing, finance, etc.

- **Performance Résumés**—This résumé type is a combination of the chronological and functional approaches. You list employment information in a chronological format, then organize the skills you've developed in each position in order to highlight your accomplishments.

- **Focused Résumés**—This is a tailor-made résumé designed for specific professions such as teachers, civil servants, computer professionals, lodging professionals, food service operators, etc. This résumé only lists those jobs you've had which directly relate to the specific area you are targeting. This format is often used by large corporations to track performance and skills within their own organization. If you are looking for promotion within a company, this format may suit your needs. This format is not as popular because it is very specific.

- **Government Résumés**—If you are interviewing for a government position or with a company that contracts with the government, you may be asked to submit a standardized résumé, laid out in a specific format. They are usually narrative in nature, and should use terms from standardized job descriptions and other government documents.

Ask the Expert - Résumé Do's and Don'ts

Q. How do I choose which organizational style to use?

A. It depends on your audience and your experience. People with limited experience and education should use the chronological layout. If you have more experience and/or education and want to emphasize your skills or coursework, use a performance résumé. That way you can list your courses and highlight skills obtained from your jobs. If you have been in the workforce for several years, and are looking to highlight your skills for a promotion or applying for a job where you are emphasizing your experience, use the functional résumé.

Q. What if I am short on education or work experience?

A. If you are coming out of college and looking for a starting position, you'll want to emphasize your coursework. Highlight the classes that related to your major and indicate the types of skills you gained from the courses. Use any community service or volunteer work you have done that may show leadership, experience, or skills. Join a professional organization that will get you connected to other people in your industry. Get teachers or others who have experienced your work to write you a letter of recommendation, highlighting what you have done.

Q. Do I put education or work experience first?

A. If you have education but limited work experience, list education first. If you have been in the workforce for several years, list experience first. If you are changing fields and your work experience doesn't relate to the area you are entering, list experience first, highlighting your transferrable skills. You decide which is stronger: your education or your work experience.

Q. Do I list everything I've done?

A. If you have limited work experience, list it all. If you have had a variety of short-term positions, list the jobs that are relevant to the position you are applying for. Some experts recommend leaving off any experiences older than 10 years, but if the experiences have value and add to your employability in the current position, go ahead and list them.

Q. What do I do if I have gaps in my résumé?

A. If you're talking about timelines where you were unemployed for a period of time, leave in the gap and be prepared to talk about it if the question arises in an interview. If you have skill gaps, where you don't have all of the qualifications for the position but you are applying anyway, you will want to emphasize your strengths and your ability to learn new skills. The cover letter that goes with the résumé may be the best place to cover this. Be sure to use keywords specific to the industry so your résumé will have a better chance of getting to the "interview" pile.

Q. What if I don't have any awards or memberships?

A. It's OK if you don't have awards or professional memberships. You can use your work experience and education to promote your abilities. It is a good idea to join a professional organization in your field in order to keep learning and growing professionally.

Many organizations have student branches for professionals just entering the field. Join the organizations that will help you to continue to learn new things and grow.

Q. Should I list my references on the résumé?

A. Most employers do not contact references until you have been interviewed and you are being considered for the position. Besides, you may need all that room to list skills gained from coursework or job experiences. Create a separate reference sheet and indicate on your résumé that your Career Portfolio and References are available upon request. Include a copy of the references in your portfolio and keep an individual copy available to give to the interviewer if it is requested.

Q. I've heard that my résumé should fit on one page. Can I go over one page in length?

A. As a general rule, if you are just out of school, you should be able to keep your résumé to one page. If you have more experience you can expand it. Even the most experienced person should keep his or her résumé to three pages. Your résumé can be longer than one page, but be sure that the information you include is a good representation of you. Today, more résumés are being sorted and processed electronically, where the computer program scans for certain keywords. You may benefit from listing key skills and abilities you have gained from your experiences, and that can take up more space.

Q. Can I use a fancy type style and paper to help my résumé stand out from the rest?

A. With many job openings generating hundreds of applications, employers are looking to technology to help them deal with the volume of applicants. They will often scan a résumé into electronic format and then use a software program to scan for certain keywords in the résumé. One of the problems with fancy type styles is that they don't scan well. The software is used to dealing with plain type styles and can mess up on fancy ones. The last thing you want is to have your résumé scanned and your name come in wrong because you have it in a funky font. The same rule goes for paper. Using paper with shaded or mottled backgrounds can cause the scanner to misread words.

Your best option is to use a readable font, on high quality white paper. Lay out your résumé with plenty of white space in an attractive format and use appropriate keywords to set your résumé apart. Check out Chapter 9, Style Guide, for more details on making your résumé look great.

 Template

Most word processing programs such as Microsoft Word and Word Perfect include templates for creating résumés. We suggest you use these templates as a starting point for creating your own résumé.

Choosing the Right Words

Regardless of the style of résumé you choose to create, you should describe the skills and experiences associated with your jobs and education. Using the right words to capture experience can sometimes be challenging. When it comes to identifying skills and items for the résumé and the career portfolio, you'll want to use a combination of action verbs and keywords. The technology of today has shifted people's thinking—while they are still looking for action-oriented people (action verbs), they are also looking for ways to quickly dial into who and what you are by descriptive things you can do. What concrete terms can be used to describe you? Focus on the skills and keyword terms that are core to your specific profession.

Add Keywords to Your Résumé

"Keywords" are those terms that cue people in to specific skills and abilities. If you've ever used a search engine on the Internet, you've used keywords. Think about your résumé as if it were a website. What terms do you want people to look for and find? A person wanting to be employed in the technology field might list the software packages he/she works in. Also include business functions such as "web design" or "meeting planning," etc. Employers use keywords to screen applicants for interviews. Make sure your résumé makes the cut.

Action verbs are used on a résumé to describe what you have done. Here are a few action verbs to get you thinking:

accomplished, advised, assessed, authorized, budgeted, completed, conducted, demonstrated, managed, encouraged, maintained, recommended, scheduled, solved, etc..

A more extensive list of action verbs is included in Chapter 10, Reference Guide, for use in your résumé to indicate the action you have completed. Use them with keywords to demonstrate your skills. As a rule, scanned résumés look more at keywords, whereas a résumé reviewed by a person tends to note the action verbs. In the following descriptions the **action verb is in bold** and the keywords are underlined:

- **Managed** a team of four documentation writers
- **Maintained** a database of 25,000 customers
- Meeting planning - Helped **plan**, **organize,** and **manage** the 1999, 2000, and 2001 Midwest CHRIE conferences - Committee member
- Webmaster - **designed** website, **maintained** online registration, **managed** conference database and registration

The Scannable Résumé

With the volume of applicants for positions, more companies are using computers to select potential candidates for the interview process. The software and scanning technology is quite advanced, and it is more cost effective than paying an employee to do the same work. With the thought in mind that your résumé may never be read by a real person, it's time to plan ahead and create a résumé that appeals to both the computer and the human reader. You can do this by using keywords and action verbs and by formatting the résumé in a way that it will be scanned easily by the computer. Here are some guidelines for making your résumé scanner friendly:

- **Use black ink on 8 1/2" x 11" white paper, printed only on one side**
- **Don't use italic or underline**
- **Use 12- to 14- pitch font size for body text and 16- to 18-pitch fonts for headings**
- **Use a non-decorative type style**
- **Place your name on each page in the header or footer**
- **Use one-inch margins all the way around the document** (During the scanning process, margins are sometimes trimmed and information could be lost with a smaller margin.)
- **Avoid using staples or folding the résumé on a line of text**
- **Avoid the use of graphics, shading, and lines**
- **Identify dates and times you are available at different contact addresses. Include E-mail addresses where possible.**
- **Use keywords** - Using the vocabulary and terminology of your industry is critical. Using terms like "dollar volume," "number of people supervised," "franchise vs. corporate owned," etc., may allow your résumé to be selected over another.

Here is a scannable performance résumé with good use of action verbs and keywords:

Shauna R. Johnson

711 Oak Street • Conner, Indiana • 47351 • Phone: 825.765.7922 • E-mail: shauy@si-net.com

Objective	Design, develop, and implement instructional programs in an adult educational setting

Summary of Skills

Communications	*Leadership*	*Computer*
Oral Presentations	Training	Windows 95 and 98
Reports	Customer Service	MS Word
Business Letters	Ordering	MS Publisher
Copy Writing	Scheduling	Page Maker
Proof Reading	Merchandising	Freehand
Editing	Displays	E-Mail
Page Layout	Management Skills	Web Navigation
Document Design	Organizational Skills	Desk Top Publishing
Interpersonal Skills	Conflict and Group Management	

Education

Expected Graduation Date • May 2000 • Indiana University East • Richmond, Indiana
BA • General Studies
> Concentration in Psychology
> Specialty in Tourism Management
>> Certificate Safe Serve Food Service Sanitation
>> Certificate Tourism Management with courses in:
Management
Marketing
Human Resource Management
Tourism
Hospitality
Sanitation

Awards

Consistently Named to the Dean's List
1997 and 1999 Nominee Student of the Year
1999 General Studies Distinguished Student
Other Awards Appear in Portfolio

Professional Experience

1997—Present   Indiana University East   Richmond, Indiana
Hospitality/Tourism Management Program Assistant • Writing Lab Tutor • Peer Mentor
Connersville Center Associate • Orientation Coordinator

> Instructing, and Tutoring Students in the Art of Note-taking, Learning Styles, Organizational Skills, Scheduling, and Other Academic Areas
> Organizing, Coordinating, and Implementing New Student Orientations
> Reviewing and Editing Student Compositions
> Reviewing Student Assignments and Portfolios
> Advising New and Returning Students in the Areas of University Resources, Scheduling, Prerequisite Courses, and Retention Issues
> Marketing and Recruiting

Collegiate Activities

1997-Present • President • Alpha Sigma Lambda Honor Society • Theta Mu Chapter
1996-Present • President • Pacesetters and Activities Council of Connersville

Community Activities

1996-1998 • Chapter Leader • Indiana Chronic Fatigue Syndrome Association • Connersville
Regular Election Poll Worker • Sheriff
Sunday School Teacher

Portfolio

Available for review

A professional résumé - skills are chunked and she has integrated keywords and action verbs to describe her experiences

New Trends in Résumés

Online Résumé Services

These days you may end up finding a job by placing your résumé in an electronic database. A growing number of services are now available which will scan in your résumé and place it on the Internet or other database services. Many of these websites are geared to people in certain industries. These are popular with employees because they can get the résumés of prospective employers who are already screened to a certain industry.

Some services will scan in your résumé and ask you to complete a brief application, including items such as salary preferences, employers, willingness to travel, distance willing to travel, etc. The service gives employers access to "at a glance" peeks at your résumé. For a fee, they will give an employer a copy of the entire résumé via fax. After that, it's up to the employer to contact you.

Some of these services will provide you with feedback on who requested your résumé and the salary ranges other professionals with similar skills are earning in the industry. They will also identify trends in professional fields, such as a need for increased computer skills for Restaurant Management.

Professional databases are available not only to college graduates, but also to professionals trying to determine the marketability of their skills. You can find these databases by browsing on the Internet using key terms such as **career placement**, **job search**, and **employment**. Within the databases, you can search for openings by experience, salary ranges, key interest areas, etc. For using these services you will sometimes pay a flat fee of $25 to $75. In other cases, your résumé is scanned in for free and the employer pays for access.

College Placement Websites

Many colleges and university placement centers have embraced the Internet and are using it to the advantage of graduates and alumni alike. Many schools keep a résumé database, whereas others are providing students with space for personal web pages. If you have the opportunity to create your own website, check out Chapter 7, The Electronic Portfolio, for tips and guidelines to creating your site.

Web Page Résumés

More people are now putting résumés online with their own web pages. The really savvy people are creating more than just résumés—they're creating on-line portfolios. It's especially critical that your résumé be well developed so you can focus the person searching your page. Links and key terms are critical. See Chapter 7, The Electronic Portfolio, for more details.

Sending Out Your Résumé

Keep in mind that your résumé is the tool that gets you an interview. Your résumé needs to represent you and should be a professional looking document. Be sure to double and triple check your résumé for typos, formatting errors, and correct information. Simple errors can show a lack of attention to details and may cause your résumé to be automatically rejected by some employers.

Cover Letters

A cover letter is sent with the résumé and should briefly explain what sets you apart from others and why you would be the best person for the job. Employers use the cover letter to check for writing style, attention to detail and tone, as well as your qualifications. Here are a few "do's" for cover letters:

- Check your spelling and grammar.
- Address the letter to the specific person who will be reviewing your letter.
- Draw attention to key summaries of your résumé.
- Explain what types of opportunities you are looking to secure.

E-Mailing Your Résumé

Occasionally you may be asked to E-mail your résumé to a prospective employer or contact at an organization. This is often the case when you have a personal contact with someone in the organization. E-mailing your résumé gives you quick strike ability. You can react faster and have your résumé on the employer's desk faster than with regular mail. Here are some general guidelines to follow when E-mailing a résumé:

- **Send your résumé as an attachment** — Send the résumé as a Word file or an Adobe PDF (Portable Document File) file so it can be printed out by the receiver.

- **Include a cover letter** — Send the cover letter as an attachment, or write your cover letter in the body of the E-mail.

- **Include your contact information in the body of the E-mail**—This way if there are any problems with the files, the receiver can get to you as quickly as possible.

- **Save your résumé in a PDF format if possible**— The receipient must have a program called Acrobat viewer on their computer. The program can be downloaded from the Internet for free. This format can be printed directly from the browser, and the document also cannot be edited or changed by anyone else. Check your computer center or Placement Office for assistance on creating PDFs.

- **Use standard fonts like Times New Roman or Arial when sending your résumé document** — If the receiver's computer doesn't have your funky font installed, your document will print with different fonts and will not look its best.

- **Use your private E-mail, not a corporate account** — Organizations have the right to monitor their employees' E-mail. If you are currently employed and looking for another job, you should correspond through a private E-mail account, not the corporate address. Do you want them knowing you're actively looking?

- **Send a hard copy of your résumé and cover letter by mail—** Follow-up your E-mail with a hard copy to reinforce your E-mail message and to serve as a backup copy.

Faxing Your Résumé

You can also respond quickly to a request by faxing your résumé to an employer. Since the quality of a fax machine copy is inferior to a printed hard copy, you should send this only at the request of the organization. Here are a few guidelines to consider when faxing a résumé:

- **Fax from a copy of your résumé printed on white paper —** Colored paper and paper with texture do not fax well and tend to be grainy and hard to read. White paper will fax better.

- **Include a cover letter —** Send the cover letter and résumé together with a cover sheet directed to the correct person.

- **Use standard fonts like Times New Roman or Arial when sending your résumé —** Again, funky fonts don't always print well on the other end of the fax machine.

- **Consider the uses of your office fax machine —** The sending fax machine produces a log of all faxes sent. It often lists the name of the organization at the receiving end of a fax. Consider carefully if you want your employer to know you're faxing things to another organization or competitor...

- **Make sure the fax goes through —** Be sure you stand at the machine until the fax has been successfully sent. If it doesn't go through or the line is busy it may drop your fax job. Wait for a confirmation statement from the fax machine.

- **Send a hard copy of your résumé and cover letter by mail—** Follow-up your fax with a hard copy to reinforce your message and to serve as a backup copy.

Your Résumé Sets the Stage

In Chapter 2 you planned out your portfolio and decided where to focus your efforts. By developing your résumé, you have identified the educational and job related experiences you want to emphasize. You have really created an overview of your portfolio, the first step to creating the finished product. Use your résumé as a guide in the next two chapters as you begin to collect and organize work samples. As you begin to sort and decide on work samples you may find that your résumé needs to be adjusted. Congratulations! You're on your way to creating a focused portfolio that will help provide backup and support to your résumé!

Related Websites

Here are just a few of the thousands of websites designed to help you create the perfect résumé. Use these sites as guidelines. Remember, you are creating a product that represents **you** to potential employers. Follow your instincts and create the résumé that feels right to you.

- **America's Job Bank** - http://www.ajb.dni.us/
- **America's Talent Bank** - http://atb.mesc.state.mi.us/
- **CareerCity** - http://www.careercity.com/
- **CareerMagazine** - http://www.careermag.com/
- **CareerMosaic** - http://www.careermosaic.com/
- **CareerPath.com** - http://www.careerpath.com/
- **CareerWeb** - http://www.careerweb.com/
- **JobBank USA** : Jobs MetaSEARCH - http://www.jobbankusa.com/search.html
- **JobTrak** - http://www.jobtrak.com/
- **Online Career Center** - http://www.occ.com/
- **Resumail** - http://www.resumail.com/
- **ResumeBlaster** - http://www.resumeblaster.com/

- **The Job Hunters Bible** - What Color Is My Parachute? - http://www.jobhuntersbible.com
- **The Monster Board** - http://www.monster.com/
- **Weddle's Web Guide** - http://www.nbew.com/
- **The Career Clinic** - http://www.thecareerclinic.com/

4 PROVING YOUR SKILLS

This chapter is all about proof. Chapters 2 and 3 helped to determine what skill areas you need to emphasize. Now we'll take that information and look at how to find, create, and select work samples, certificates, letters of recommendation, skill sets, and support materials which make up the heart of your portfolio. In this chapter you'll find the details on:

- finding and choosing work samples.
- asking for and using letters of recommendation.
- creating works in progress.
- working with skill sets.
- using certifications, diplomas, degrees, and awards.
- using community service to prove your skills.
- using academic plan of study and faculty/employer bios.
- creating the reference materials needed to support your portfolio.

Look at the Big Picture

Decide what skill areas you want to emphasize, whether it's Communications, Management, Accounting, Restaurant Management, Computer Skills, Graphics, Menu Development, Leadership, Auditing, or Public Relations. Try to have three to five different areas. Then select work samples that correspond to these areas. If you don't have very many work samples, you may find yourself creating categories to support your samples. It's important to make sure that the samples you use support your goals and will show your best work.

Work Samples

Work samples make up the major portion of the portfolio and become the most powerful part of your sales pitch.

Work samples are proof of your knowledge and skills. When assembling your portfolio for an interview, you can customize your work samples to match the skills needed for the position. You can "wow" a potential employer by showing examples that clearly demonstrate skills he or she want's to see. Work samples also add to your credibility. Instead of just telling someone what you have done, you can show examples.

Sources of Work Samples

Common sources for work samples include:

- **Classroom projects from your major core courses during school.**
- **Materials you have generated while on the job or on an internship or co-op.**
- **Materials completed in community service projects or professional memberships.**

Class Assignments

Projects you developed to fulfill course requirements are a great source of work samples. The grade you earned on the project is usually not included, but could be brought up as a point of discussion in the interview. Some examples include:

- **Real life simulations.**
- **A feasibility study you generated in a marketing class.**
- **The menu you designed for your menu design project or capstone food course.**
- **A business plan you developed.**
- **An advertising campaign you developed as a team effort.**
- **Office or facility designs.**

Anything you create that shows your skill in a particular area can be used as a work sample. If the physical evidence is too big to fit in the portfolio (like a poster or diagram) take a picture of the item and include the photo.

The more details you can give about the project, the better. You may want to include some of the following items for each project sample:

- The faculty assignment sheet—you may have to re-key it so that it is presentable.
- Table of Contents for the entire project.
- Names of people working on the project.
- Assignment summaries.
- Why it was generated, the purpose it served.
- Executive summaries where possible.
- Financial summaries where appropriate.
- Pictures.
- Multimedia summaries.
- What you learned from the project.
- Any prerequisites to this assignment.

Ask the Expert - I got rid of all my projects...

Q: I'm a senior - I did a lot of projects, but I've thrown them out. What can I put in my portfolio to show my experiences?

A: It's always frustrating when you realize you had great projects that would show experience but you've cleared your "clutter" and thrown them away. Check and see if your instructor has an assignment sheet for the project which could be included in the portfolio. You could also write up a project summary; list the assignment, what you created, and what you learned from it. Keep the project summary sheet to a single page. Depending on the type of project, you may also have photos that could be used.

On-the-Job Samples, Co-Op Projects, or Internship Projects

Having a hard time coming up with work samples? Take a look at the things you do on the job and consider the things you create and work with on a daily basis that show your experience. Consider these work sample ideas:

- **Sections of the employee handbook.**
- **Departmental operating procedures.**
- **Programs or systems created.**
- **Campaigns created or advanced.**
- **Market research techniques.**
- **Promotional materials.**
- **Job projects such as employee newsletters.**
- **Special events created.**
- **Multimedia presentations created.**

Ask the Expert - I need some experience!

Q: I recently obtained my diploma and graduated with honors, but in my field there aren't many jobs open. Those that are advertising want someone with experience. So far, I have my résumé posted on several job search web sites, but that hasn't been too productive either. Any advice?

A: It seems you have a lot to offer. There are a couple of ways to address the work experience problem:
1. Seek out a paid internship with a respected company. Go in with an educational contract where you want to have specific work experience to document. You need at least six-months experience and often times this can be worked around another position as long as you are up front as to what you want to accomplish. 2. Find any class projects you generated which could serve as work samples in your

career portfolio. 3. You need to be prepared for more than just the obvious fields where you can use your skills. Determine your transferable skills and find out other industries that need people with these skills. The hospitality, lodging, and restaurant management industry is a field where people from many different backgrounds can apply their skills. Broaden your search. Consider joining a professional association where you can network and become known- it adds to your credibility while you build work experience.

Community Service Projects

Community involvement is a great source of work samples that are often overlooked by people as they pull together their portfolios. Service samples may be written projects or pictures of your involvement in community service. Examples include:

- **The poster and picture of the "Brotherhood Tree of Giving" you designed for the lobby of a hotel.**
- **The grant proposal you helped create for a day-care facility.**
- **A flyer you created for the June mailing.**
- **A picture of your team building a house.**
- **A photo of you working in a soup kitchen.**
- **The menu you developed for the PTA dinner**
- **The menu and production plan for the catered dinner for 80.**

Include the following information for each community service sample:

- A summary sheet of what you accomplished.
- Results of the project.
- Who helped you.
- A photo if appropriate

If your community service samples relate to one of your skill areas, you may choose to put your sample there. If your service experience doesn't relate, you should create a separate tabbed section for community service.

Putting It Together

Work samples are the dynamic portion of your portfolio. As you prepare for different job interviews, your portfolio needs to be adjusted as well. You may need to change the work samples you show to demonstrate specific abilities that are desired by the company. You need to evaluate your portfolio before each interview to make sure it fits the prospective employer's needs. Selecting the correct work samples and keeping them organized for instant access is very important. Follow these guidelines to help you in selecting your samples:

- **How to select the best work samples**— Ask yourself the following questions about each sample:
  - What will this work demonstrate—skills, competencies, or achievement of goals?
  - Is this my best work?
  - Does it show mastery?
  - Am I proud of this sample . . . all or part of it?
- **Include a sample, not the whole project**—Try to limit yourself to a maximum of 20 pages per project. People don't want to read everything.
- **Offer the full project** —Add a line on a work sample overview card offering the full project:

  Full project available upon request

- **Identify people who contributed to the project**—When presenting work samples, clearly identify its purpose and everyone who has contributed to the sample.
- **When in doubt, leave it out**— Never include a work sample that you are not proud to be associated with, now or in the future. Remember that more is not necessarily better; in fact, it could be the "kiss of death."
- **Use a photo summary**— A photo summary of your work may be the best way to relay a work experience. Create photos which show summaries of your work, not just the physical environment. Include pictures of yourself in action with the project.

- **Make it look good**— Select the best way to present your work samples: through text or photos. (See Chapter 9, A Matter of Style, for more information).

- **Use grouped sheet protectors for projects**— You can purchase special sets of 5 or 10 interconnected sheet protectors. Use these to keep an entire project sample together so you can easily switch out projects in the portfolio when customizing it to the employer.

- **Pay attention to confidentiality**— Materials generated on the job are usually the property of the company you were working for at the time you created the material. When you display or show that material, be sure to recognize the owner. If you have signed a confidentiality agreement with a company, you should not include their work in your portfolio.

It's Confidential...

John included materials from his job in his work samples and indicated on the sample cards that it was used with permission. He interviewed with his portfolio but didn't get the job. When he asked the interviewer for feedback, the interviewer had felt that the samples were confidential, and if he was showing samples in an interview, how would he handle confidentiality on the job?

Keeping Track of Your Work Samples

- **Have a schedule for updating your collection of work samples**—Develop a routine for collecting materials. If you are in school, you may choose midterm and final exam time to stop and consider which, if any, of your work should be saved for your files. On the job, make a 30- to 60-minute appointment with yourself once every quarter to take time to reflect on your work over the past months. You should consider completed reports, projects, awards, achievements, or project summaries.

- **Keep track of your work samples**—Get a large plastic tote with hanging folders. You should keep original copies of projects, letters of recommendations, letters of accommodation, or certificates of achievement or degrees. You don't need to spend lots of time arranging it; you just need a designated place to keep your materials.

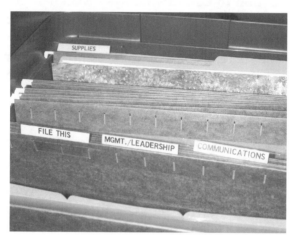

Use a tote with files to store your work samples and supplies

- **Include the correct work samples**—The work samples you include in your portfolio will vary, based on the needs of the potential employer. You should have a collection of different work samples stored in your tote or filing cabinet. Each sample should be in its own set of sheet protectors, so you can quickly swap out appropriate work samples as needed.

- **Organize work samples into the appropriate skill areas**—Work samples should be clustered by major skill areas. You determine these skill areas. Each skill area will have its own tabbed section in the portfolio. Each skill area should contain work samples that emphasize that particular area. See the section on Skill Sets in this chapter for more information on organizing the skills area section of your portfolio.

- **Organize work samples within a skill area**—The organization and flow of work samples will vary with each sample. Try to break up text and photos so that the arrangement creates growing interest and peaks curiosity. You may want to organize your work samples in a flow that will show growth or chronological advancement.

- **Use work sample overview cards**— An work sample overview card is a small card containing a brief summary of the work sample. It is placed inside the page protector of the first page of your sample, and helps the reader remember what he or she is looking at and why. We recommend that you create cards for each work sample using a blank sheet of standard size business cards. Format the page on your computer, and include the following information:

  - Title of the project.
  - Purpose of the project.
  - Date of work.
  - Who worked with you.
  - What skills are demonstrated using keywords.

Sample:

> **Marketing Feasibility Study for Franchise Hotel**
>
> Fall Term 2000
>
> Group project - Anna Williams, Mark Warner, Karen Hall, & David Morrow
>
> Analysis—Competitive, customer, SWOT

 Template

Use the template on the enclosed disk to create your own work sample overview cards. **(Work Sample Overview Cards.doc)**

Letters of Recommendation

Letters of recommendation from employers, instructors, etc., can provide additional proof of your abilities. Letters provide personal references from people who have seen you perform. You may need to rely more on letters of recommendation when you don't have many work samples, or when the type of work you do doesn't facilitate written samples.

You should solicit letters from people who know you and/or your work personally. Instructors, supervisors, owners, presidents, and guests—all can be appropriate references. Whoever you choose should be familiar with your work and be able to judge perfor-mance and competency. You should be proud to be associated with these people. If you don't like them, they probably don't like you, and you don't want a letter from them.

Asking for a Letter

- You should request your letter of recommendation in writing long before you need it.

- Your letter needs to help guide the person writing the recommendation to focus his or her letter on key skills and areas of your personality that you want addressed.

- Ask for the letter while you are close to the event or you still have an opportunity for contact with the person.

- You should always allow two to three weeks for receiving the letter, as people tend to get busy. It is appropriate to follow up with them a week after your request.

To ask for a recommendation, remember to start with courtesy and manners; say Please and Thank You frequently, and in a heartfelt way. Remember, these people hold your success in the palm of their hands. Your goal, the purpose of a letter, is to document your performance, have your achievement recognized, and/or to have your abilities summarized. **Most people write lousy letters of recommendation.** They tend to make the letters too general or generic. You need to help the person you choose to write the letter. When writing your letter, begin by telling the person the purpose of the letter: for your portfolio, for graduate school, for a press release etc. Then, dial in your reference by giving them a list of traits, skills or attributes you want addressed. Here are some examples:

- Leadership.
- Ability to work in groups.
- Ability to self motivate.
- Ability to meet guest needs.
- Ability to complete work.
- Ability to supervise.
- Management skills.
- Creativity.
- People skills.

The Perfect Letter

The letter should be on official letterhead, should have an ink signature, and should not be folded. The recommendation letter you receive should be addressed as "Dear Future Employer." Do not use the generic, open-ended salutations such as "To Whom It May Concern" . . . or "Dear Sir or Madame." It should also include background information on how the reference knows you and how long you have been associated with the organization or project. He or she should explain how long you have been associated and in what capacity.

Don't be afraid to proof their work. If you find a mistake, be humble and ask for a correction.

Letters of recommendation will go in one of three places in the portfolio—work sample documentation, professional service/membership, and/or the community service. If the letter is comprehensive, discussing two or more of these sections, include it in the work samples and refer to it in the other area. A sample request letter is shown on the next page.

Sample Request Letter

Inside Address

Today's date

Dear Professor Brush:

I was a student of yours last term in your Hospitality Senior Seminar class. I earned an A in your class, so you probably remember me. I will be graduating in May, and I am currently working on assembling my career portfolio. Could you please write a letter of recommendation addressing the following skills:

- My ability to work in groups.
- My ability to do presentations.
- My ability to perform academically.
- My ability to do electronic spreadsheets.
- My ability to read an income statement.

It would also be helpful if you could indicate how long you have known me and on what occasions you have worked with me. I would also appreciate it if you could address the letter to "Dear Future Employer."

I would greatly appreciate receiving this letter within the next two weeks. Please call or E-mail me and let me know when it would be convenient for me to pick up the letter. It would be helpful if I could pick up an unfolded letter. Thank you very much for your consideration and all your help. Please feel free to call me if you have any questions.

Sincerely,

David Morrow

David Morrow
1996 W. Peach Blossom Rd.
Warwick, RI 02888
(401)555-6804 - Home phone
e-mail: davidm@machoo.ocean.com

Template

A sample recommendation request letter is included on the accompanying diskette. Use it as a starting point for writing your own letters. (**Recommendation request.doc**)

Transferable Skills

Transferable skills are skills that you can use in a variety of different industries and settings. A person with management skills can successfully transition from a career in banking to a career in insurance. Good computer skills can be used to develop spreadsheets for a restaurant or track medical records in an office. Begin to identify your skills and how they can be used in different ways. What else can you bring to the table in terms of expertise? Are you a subject matter expert in any fields? The ability to speak Spanish could be the asset that sets you apart from other candidates and gets you the job. As our economy becomes more global, many companies are looking to their employees for more than the requirements of the job. Having transferable skills can lead to more opportunities and the ability to transition to different jobs as the market shifts.

Ask the Expert - I'm looking for a career change

Q. After 15 years selling print advertising in the Northwest I am thinking about a career change. I love advertising and helping people write ads and seeing them work, but there are not a lot of venues in the area where I live. Should I stay in sales and just change to a different product or try a complete shift to doing something different?

A. It sounds like you have a lot of skills and a love of the type of work you are in. A couple of questions to think about: Do you want to continue to work in the same region where you are now situated? Do you know why you want a change? Here are a couple of things to consider--first, you already have connections with the infrastructure where you are; use this as an asset in looking and connecting with another position. Second, 15 years experiences in the marketing/advertising field are very transferable to other positions such as the e-commerce marketing that is rapidly growing, or in immigrant marketing in which we are seeing growth throughout the country. Collect and choose work samples from clients you have had and the behind-the-scenes processes you take people through. Make sure you abide by confidentiality agreements. Consider tabbed sections of your portfolio in the key areas of communication, advertising, and management or leadership.

Ask the Expert - Blending Skills

Q. I would like to combine my skills and advance. My first career was computer programming and my second career is paralegal. Are there any fields of work that this combination would be valuable to?

A. There are several career options that are key to a career match. In your case—and with the technology needs of today--you are very marketable. You have content expertise in two areas--computer programming and the paralegal field. There are positions in the legal field; there are also a great deal of computer opportunities in the area of web design. There are also good matches in the areas of advocacy work, especially where you can integrate your programming abilities. Focus your job search on the Internet and in the local geographic areas where you want to be employed. Be sure to promote the programming skills you have via a career portfolio. List all languages you program in as well as the applications you have had. Break out your paralegal skills in terms of research and content areas in the fields you have worked on or specialized in. Concentrate on taking these two distinct fields and partnering them via transferable skills into the career match.

Works in Progress

This is a place to list projects on which you are currently working. You may choose to show parts or modules that are completed enough to demonstrate a skill, competency, or achievement. This section may be very short. It should be clearly labeled "Works in Progress," and can be placed at the beginning of the work samples. You may want to use a bulleted list. During an interview you may refer to this list of current projects after you have discussed your work samples. It can serve to transition the interviewer or supervisor into more questions. Your list should include:

- The expected completion date.
- Whom the work is for.
- What skills or competencies it demonstrates.

Skill Sets

What Are Skill Sets?

In some professions, you just may not have a lot of physical work samples available. A listing of your skills and how well you can do them can be used in your portfolio to demonstrate your skills and abilities. A **skill set** is a list of related skills grouped together. The look and feel of a skill set will vary depending on where you got it from. Many organizations and professions have developed skill sets for their particular fields. If you can't find any, you can always create your own skill sets.

Skill sets are not only a list of your abilities, but they also show the level of your abilities. Skills and competencies should be graded by ability. Many skill sets will work with each skill or competency, using three levels of ability:

Awareness—Has awareness of the knowledge/skill, and has completed the task at least once.

Practicing—Is able to follow a guide to complete a task.

Mastery—Is able to consistently perform the task without effort.

The following pages show a skill set created to track computer competencies:

Computers & Related Technologies

Awareness	Practicing	Mastery
Has awareness of the knowledge/skill, and/or has completed the task at least once.	Is able to follow a guide to complete the task.	Is able to consistently perform the task without effort.

Is able to load software.

print name signature date	print name signature date	print name signature date

Is able to do file management in a Windows environment.

print name signature date	print name signature date	print name signature date

Is able to create and send E-mail.

print name signature date	print name signature date	print name signature date

Is able to complete work using a word processing package.

print name	print name	print name
signature	signature	signature
date	date	date

Is able to complete work using electronic spreadsheets.

print name	print name	print name
signature	signature	signature
date	date	date

Is able to complete work using presentation software.

print name	print name	print name
signature	signature	signature
date	date	date

Is able to access the Internet and the World Wide Web using a browser and/or specific address.

print name	print name	print name
signature	signature	signature
date	date	date

Is able to send files via modem.

print name	print name	print name
signature	signature	signature
date	date	date

 Template

A blank skill set is included on the accompanying diskette. Use it as a starting point for creating your own skill sets. (**Skillset.doc**)

The style of the skill set shown above allows you to track your progress on achieving your goals and increasing your skill levels. This skill set features space for a professional or educator to sign off on your level of ability. It is important that you take responsibility for getting your skills measured and signed-off on. This is especially critical if you do not have a lot of work samples to support those skills. It is always more difficult to get a signature after the employment or class is over, since the person being asked to sign off may not have as clear a memory of the work. Be sure to request biographical information at the time of signature so you can include the information on a Faculty and Employer Biography sheet.

Creating Your Own Skill Sets

Getting started is easy. . . but takes some time.

- **Use job descriptions to identify skills you want to have—** Not all job descriptions are well written; however, there are usually key abilities identified in the text. Shop through the job requirements and evaluate your skills against those, looking for terminology. In fact, a really great way to self-evaluate your own skills is to write the job description for your ideal position and then check if you meet the qualifications. The Career Development office at your local community college, university, or professional association may be of some assistance if you are not quite sure where to look for job descriptions.

- **Use the "Want Ads" or job postings to identify and check skills**—Wants ads in the newspaper or on the Internet tend to be brief because they are paid for by the word. However, this does not devalue the interesting information about the jobs that are available. Look at the skills, written and implied. Often times it is right in front of you. Check the Sunday papers and the Tuesday edition of *The Wall Street Journal* for job advertisements.

Now expand and refine this list of skills . . .

- **List the things you have done on the job**—If the majority of your work experience is as an hourly employee (line-level) then you need to reflect on a "day in your life." If the majority of your work experience is as a supervisor then you need to reflect on a "week in your life." If the majority of your work experience is as a manager then you need to reflect on a "month in your life." What is this reflect stuff? List all the things you do in the course of a day . . . week . . . month. This usually covers your routine skills. Break your time down so that you can clearly think through the entire period of time. Your list should be of tasks and activities that you do. Try to be very specific; rather than just saying, "as a supervisor I work with people to prepare food for the restaurant," consider also your responsibility for sanitation, coaching employees, and ensuring the standards of the operation. Can you do each person's job if asked? Many times we underestimate all the skills and tasks that we do in a day.

- **List unique skills**—Things special to the position, those things you get asked to do because you are better at it than others. Focus on your creative skills, your problem solving skills, and your ability to do several things at once.

- **List your generalizable skills**—Those which can be used in many different positions. Consider your technology skills; more and more positions are specifically asking you to prove your computer skills and specific software expertise. Some companies are even giving skill tests to verify your abilities.

Get A Head Start...
Create your Skill Sets in School or on the Job

Customize your skill sets based on your coursework—While you are in school, take time at the beginning of each term to review the skills and competencies you expect to secure, refine, or learn about in each course. At the end of the project or class, you will have ability at the Awareness, Practicing, or Mastery levels. Imagine going into a class knowing what you want to get out of it, and working with the instructor to create your own learning plan. You want to be in a position to be proactive rather than reactive to your education. This keeps you from being a "passive user" of the educational system. (Remember to keep good work samples for possible use later.)

Professionals on the job—At the beginning of a job or review period, you should clearly decide what skills you have, need, or want to prove, and which ones you want to develop during the next year. You need to give yourself enough structure so that you can grow within the company and as a professional in your field. Consider incorporating your skill needs into your performance goals for the year. This is a good way to strategically organize yourself, especially if you make sure your goals and the company's goals interface or map back to each other.

Certifications, Diplomas, Degrees, or Awards

Remember, you need to prove the things you have done. Professional certificates related to areas of specialty, such as Novell certification, training certification, continuing education, workshops attended, distinctions, or accommodations are appropriate items to place in your portfolio. Here are some tips for using certificates and awards:

- **Include a copy of the certificate**—Include a quality photocopy or scanned image of the certificate or diploma as proof and verification. Don't include the original.

- **Include information about the organization presenting the certificate**—The certificate should be dated and have information about the organization. If it does not, add a page with the following items:
  - Name.
  - Address and phone number of the organization.
  - Any certification or licensing numbers given.

- **Place the most recent items first**—If you have any citations (not speeding or parking tickets!) for service, include them here in reverse chronological order with most current items coming first. For example, if you received the customer service award at work last year, and you received Dean's List this term—place the Dean's List before the customer service award.

- **Be selective**—What goes in here? Everything? No. Show items that will be of interest to your future employer. Do your homework on the interests of the organization with which you are applying or currently working for today. Remember that more is not necessarily better.

 Bright Idea!

Use color copies of originals and keep the original in a safe place. NEVER put the original copy of a project or certificate in your portfolio!

Community Service

There ARE Other Ways to Get Experience

You have not really worked in the area the potential employers are looking for . . . what can you do? Volunteer. People who are not actively in the workforce or those people who have been out for a while can use their volunteer projects as a way to demonstrate skills and secure proof, without having held employment. Go to an organization and offer your services free of charge. Start a project and see it through to the end. Be sure to make it clear that all you want is a letter documenting your time and skills. Then have some fun and test drive, develop or refine your skills.

Women or men who have stayed at home for a couple of years with their children often times feel their skills are rusty. Prior to entering the workforce, allow some time to do some structured volunteering. It could be as a fund raiser or a kitchen supervisor at the YMCA. Seek out a not-for-profit organization and offer your professional skills. It doesn't matter if you are a mechanic, a cook, a graphic artist, or an accountant—offer the skills you feel you need help documenting. One woman was let go from a full-time marketing position because she didn't have the skills that were required in her changing job. While unemployed, she volunteered in the community, handling the marketing responsibilities for a local non-profit organization. She used this experience to secure the skills her employer was looking for and was hired back. She used community service as a way of building her skills and proving her abilities.

In a recent meeting of industry recruiters, several said they look specifically for candidates with community service in their background. They believe individuals who volunteer will be willing to stay a little longer to get the project done; it signals an individual who is interested in giving back and not just taking from the community—even the corporate community. Additionally, community service is another way to create positive public relations. Sometimes, people are hired because of their volunteer connections and earned respect in the local or regional community. Other employers will require employees to do some community service such as Big Brother, Big Sister, little league coach, city council members, or serve as the Cancer Society or Heart Association chairperson.

Citizenship, ethics, and one's ability to balance his or her life is becoming more important. Volunteerism shows that you have a strategy for coping with on-the-job stress. Often times recruiters are looking for ways of seeing balance in your life. Community service is one way to demonstrate this.

- **It is appropriate to show work developed while serving with or on community organizations or associations.** Examples might include photos of events you assisted with, copies of programs you helped develop or deliver, samples of any of the brochures, bylaws, or organizational pieces you developed. Remember, the organizations you associate with are a reflection on you—choose causes you are proud to be associated with over time.

- **As your career progresses, you need to keep your samples up to date.** Select your most significant contributions as well as those most current from the last 18 months.

Include pictures of your involvement in community service

Don't underestimate this section of your portfolio. Here is your opportunity. The person reading your portfolio now has the chance to ask questions about you, your values and beliefs. Be sure you associate with causes you can support. It's important to understand the mission statement of the organization even if it's not printed on the brochure. Be prepared to answer questions about your service and about the association or organization.

Academic Plan of Study

You may be asking why you need to include an academic plan of study. The answer is really quite logical—you want to promote all the specialized education and/or training you have received. It also helps a potential employer or current employer distinguish between your background and that of other people in the position. Your plan of study defines the courses you took to complete your degree. Remember that each school, college, or university has a distinct curriculum—you want your program to be known.

Look to course catalogs and transcripts for copies of your plan of study. Transcripts give course titles and grades; if your grades are not that great, don't volunteer the transcript. You should, however, indicate that it is available upon request. You can also use the description/presentation in the school bulletin or catalog. You need to show all your courses in your major and related area. Be sure to include the pages with the program, department, and degree description, as well as the title page and the date. You will find all of this especially helpful if you ever go back to school for an advanced degree.

Before you leave your school, get 10 copies of your transcript and find the copy of the course catalog that governed your degree. You may have to go back to your freshman boxes to find it. Keep the catalog or bulletin in a safe place, since these are often expensive to get if you need them in a hurry.

It may be appropriate to include the course descriptions from key classes. You may possibly need to scan the information. Be sure to cite the date of the program and version of the catalog.

In an interview, the academic plan of study section is usually only referred to if needed and may even be overlooked when the person considering you is reviewing your portfolio. You need to have it in your portfolio, just in case.

Faculty and Employer Biographies

Faculty and employer bios are used to give you credibility. The person who signed your skill set sheets or letters of recommendation is giving his or her word that you have certain abilities. The faculty/employer bio sheet gives the interviewer background on who these people are and how they know you.

A faculty/employer bio sheet should include the following information:

- Name and Job Title.
- Organization.
- Contact Information including Address, Phone/Fax/E-mail.
- Areas of Specialty.
- Date.

- The arrangement of bios should be chronological. It is not necessary to repeat a bio for someone, unless he or she has been promoted during the signature periods of your skill sets.

- The bio sheet is placed under its own tabbed section in the portfolio, following Skill Areas and Works in Progress. This information can often be standardized and printed on labels.

 Template

A faculty and employer bio sheet is included on the included diskette. (**Faculty_Employer bios.doc**)

References

You will need three to five references that an employer can check. You should include character, academic, and employment references:

- **Character**—Someone you've worked with in the community, such as church, synagogue or mosque, not-for-profit organizations, clubs, and/or associations all can provide good character references.

- **Academic**—Professors, teachers, counselors, coaches, and people who know your academic abilities can provide academic references.

- **Employment**—Supervisors, managers, human resource people at your current and previous positions can provide employment references.

It is never appropriate to use a peer, a subordinate, or a family member as a reference.

Sample Reference Sheet:

David Morrow - References

Mr. Richard Brush
Lodging Department Chair
Hospitality College
Johnson & Wales University
8 Abbott Park Place
Providence, RI 02903
(401) 598-1000
Fax: (401)598-2000
E-mail: dbrush@laode.com
Home: (401) 555-2911 (hours: 6 p.m. to 9 p.m.)
(Academic Reference, Club Advisor)

Monsignor Robert McCaffrey
Providence Catholic Diocese
8800 Cathedral Square
Providence, RI 02903
Office: (401) 452-5938
Fax: (401) 452- 5937
(Personal Reference, Community Service)

Ms. Fran Bahmer
General Manager
Heartland Catering
RR1, Box 200
Bloomington, IL 61701
Office: (309) 663-1105
Fax: (309) 663-1106
(Employment Reference, Supervisor for three years; summer employment)

October, 2000

Include the person's name, full title, work address, work phone, fax, E-mail, and, if given permission, the person's home phone. Arrange all references on one page, and signal at the bottom of the reference the skills, competencies, or achievements the person can address. If you have more than three references, set up the page in two columns.

You should be certain that each of your references has a copy of your résumé and copies of work samples referred to them. As long as you keep them as a reference, you should forward them a copy of your résumé each time it is updated. Send each of your references a copy, highlighting the changes.

  Template

A reference sheet is included on the diskette. (**References.doc**)

Proving Your Worth

Your work samples and support materials make up the largest portion of your portfolio. Take the time to save certificates, samples, and projects as you acquire them. Get into the habit of looking at your work and looking for samples. Take advantage of the moment and take photos of events and projects. Print just one more copy of that report and throw it into your portfolio file. If you don't have many work samples, request letters or recommendations or use skill sets to prove your worth. Once you have these elements together for your portfolio, you're almost ready to begin assembly. The next chapter will look at ways to use the portfolio to track certifications and will examine ways to show your commitment to your own professional growth.

5 YOUR COMMITMENT TO PERSONAL GROWTH

Employers want to know that you are committed to the job and to the company. They also want to see you grow and expand professionally because it's good for business. Having a plan for your own professional development and growth in your field shows your commitment to yourself and your career. Most people achieve professional growth through professional memberships and certifications.

Professional Memberships and Services

Professional memberships and services show your commitment to the field and demonstrates how you will keep up with the growing and changing knowledge/skills in the field. You should be carrying at least one professional membership at all times.

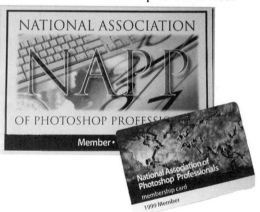

Professional memberships show your desire to grow in your career

What professional groups should you belong to? You'll find many professional groups outside your company. Join professional organizations related to your area of business rather than those that are merely social organizations. Seeking out leadership roles in a professional organization is one way to demonstrate your management and leadership abilities. Professional memberships are usually listed under a separate tabbed area in your portfolio, and are usually no more than two to four pages in length. You should include the following information:

- **A list of organizations to which you belong.**
- **The date you joined.**
- **Offices, boards, or committees on which you've served.**
- **Appropriate letters of accomplishment.**
- **Photographs of events or copies of programs where you have provided a presentation or service where appropriate.**
- **Provide proof of your membership**—Use a membership card or a letter from the president of the organization as proof of your membership. If your membership card is your canceled check, use the letter instead.
- **Spell out the name of the organization, don't just use its abbreviation.** Listing a membership in the NRA could be referring to the National Restaurant Association or the National Rifle Association.

Sample:

Professional Memberships

- CMA (Club Managers of America) —Member since 1997.
- Marketing Committee Chair—1998-Present.
- Toastmasters, since 1996.

 Template

Use the template on the enclosed disk to create your own membership listing. (**Memberships.doc**)

Using the Portfolio to Track Certifications & Professional Development

As we said in the first chapter, a portfolio is a great tool for managing information. The portfolio is the perfect place to store all the certificates, checklists, and plans necessary for many certification programs. Depending on your certification process, you may have a structured set of materials that you can put into the portfolio where you can list or mark down what you have accomplished to date. If no formal plan fits, you can create your own forms and lists to track your progress. As you obtain new skills, add them to your portfolio or check them off your list.

Ask the Expert - Do I need Certification?

Q. Currently I m working with a system integration company as a sales guy. I'm an Arts graduate with an MBA in Marketing. I have almost two years of experience in IT industry. Since I don't have any technical background, I sometimes feel the urgency of having some certification in IT. Please advise me: Should I go for any sort of certification at all that could give a boost to my career?

A. Certification is a definite boost to a career. In the field of technology, certificates can make a $15-20,000 difference in salary per year. Make sure you understand why you are pursuing the certification and choose the right program. Look at the jobs people with these certifications are doing. Is this what you want to do? The best way to determine which certification program would meet your needs is to do two things— 1) Look on the internet and local paper in the wants ads and analyze the job ads--what type of qualifications are they asking for? 2) Connect with the local professional IT group in your area and see what types of certifications the members have and value. Start putting together work samples--they will

help you when you do get to the interviewing process. A certification can assist in increasing your
starting salary.

Be sure to collect work samples as you complete your certification. Projects, letters of recommendation, and skill sets help document your experience. If you are in the process of completing a certification, make sure one of your career goals is the completion of the certification program.

Keep in mind that certifications and advanced degrees can take a considerable amount of time and effort to complete. Ask yourself some of these questions to determine why you want the degree:

- Does your future career path require a certificate or degree to open the door?

- Will your salary increase enough to pay for the advanced cost of education over time?

- Do you have a passion for learning? Advanced degrees, while more pleasurable because of the focus, often require great amounts of timely work.

Ask the Expert - Paying for Certification

Q. I want to re-focus my career and get two certifications. They are expensive and I want to find an
employer who will cover the cost of certification.
How can I do this?

A. The answer is two fold—chunk the certifications &
show your employer what is in it for him or her. There
are a couple ways to handle the discussion. The first
is to generate a sound list of benefits to the
employer. Develop your career portfolio to prove
what a good match you are for the certification.
Offer to guarantee two years of service--that is to
say you will not seek outside employment within that
time. If you do, you will repay the amount spent on
your certification. Also be prepared for discussing
your career path as you see it with this company and

what the cost benefit of you earning these certifications can be for the company. Consider things like saving outside consultant fees and increased efficiency. Work the numbers on your hourly rate and the estimated time saving. Always wear glasses that will help your employer see what is in it for him/her. Present your proposal in writing without the guarantee repayment for of two years. Talk to the person who controls the money for professional development. Start again by showing the gain to the company, how it fits into the company's strategic plan, and how you will be greatly improved as an employee.

Memberships and certifications can help prove to an employer that you are serious about your job and your career. Take some time to look at your "master plan" and decide how this can all work together to advance your career. Education is valued, and when packaged correctly, you can open many doors and have fun.

6 THE ASSEMBLY

Assembling the Portfolio

OK, you have all your stuff in piles and files—now what? Remember that the first chapter of this book gave you the big picture view on the portfolio. Chapters 2 to 5 gave you the gory details of each section in the portfolio (perhaps even more than you really wanted to know). This chapter will take you from the pieces to the whole finished product. You won't be ready to assemble until you first gather, sort, secure, and update your materials. We'll also take a look at special tips for assembling a Performance Portfolio for use in job reviews or promotion interviews.

Here are the five major steps to assembling your portfolio:

Step 1: Gather your supplies and documents.

Step 2: Sort and organize your work samples.

Step 3: Put them all together.

Step 4: Develop support materials.

Step 5: Check it out - Proof it, test it...

Step 1 . . . Things to Gather

If you haven't already done so, read Chapters 1 to 5 of this book. Know what your goals and objectives are and how you plan to use your portfolio. Next, bring to one central location all your collected materials—consciously collect:

- **Portfolio supplies**—(see Chapter 1, "What Supplies Do I Need to Get Started?" or Chapter 10, Resource Guide)

- **Your résumé.**
- **Your work philosophy.**
- **Your professional goals.**
- **Your box of work samples. . .** (Are there any old papers or projects that you can find or copy?)
- **Certifications.**
- **Degrees or diplomas.**
- **Thank you letters or letters of recommendation**
- **Skill sets with signatures.**
- **Faculty/employer bios.**
- **Academic plans of study.**
- **Professional membership cards and service samples.**
- **Certification checklists**
- **Community service accommodations or service samples.**
- **List of references.**
- **And don't forget—your best friend.**

Step #1 - Gather your materials ... and a friend

Assemble Your Portfolio BEFORE You Need It!

With all the work involved in creating a portfolio it's easy to put it off until another day. If you decide not to choose this option of working in advance on the portfolio, please refer to the Emergency "I Need the Portfolio Now" instructions in Chapter 10, Resource Guide. We promise you'll need them. Even the authors of this book have had to choose between sleep and finishing a portfolio. Be prepared to clean off a big section of the floor for the assembly. If the floor cramps your style, use a table or large desk—just be prepared to find some space on a flat surface.

Step 2 . . . Sorting and Organizing Work Samples

Set Up Your Tabbed Areas

Use the job description, classified ad, and any other knowledge you have of the company or the position to prioritize the skills you will emphasize in your portfolio. Begin by selecting three to five main skill areas you want to emphasize and create a tab for each. Select categories which you can support with work samples. If you are a Business major, for example, your tabs might be Management, Finance, and Communication. Now is the time to decide what other tabbed areas beyond work samples you want to use.

Step 2 - Select tabs that represent you

Remember, this is your portfolio. You need to select the tabbed areas that best represent you. If you don't have any community service experiences, don't create a tab for it and then leave it blank. Don't struggle to find some activity or event to include just so you can write up two lines on a page. If you don't have it, don't include it! Play to your strengths. If you have only one sample for an area, consider grouping it with another sample from a different area and make a tab to reflect this. If you've been on the job for 10 years, you probably don't need to include a tab for Academic Plan of Study. If you can only come up with two really good tabbed areas, don't struggle to find a third and then include marginal samples. You are designing this portfolio to show off your strengths. Choose your tabbed areas to reflect this.

Selecting Samples

How do you decide which samples to use? Consider first the needs of the employer and look at the job ad to see what samples would be most effective. When sorting work and service samples, ask yourself:

- **Which skills are the organization looking for in this position?**
- **What is your best work?**
- **Which samples show the most skills and competencies?**
- **Which work samples are the most interesting to you?**
- **Which work samples use more than text as an exhibit? Do any include pictures?**
- **Can you talk about your sample?**

 Bright Idea!

Remember to select your best samples!

Consider using some of the following items as demonstrations of your skills and competency:

- **class projects**
- **projects or reports demonstrating organization and professionalism**
- **writing samples**
- **computing samples**
- **team efforts**
- **certificates from workshops**
- **performance appraisals (include internships/co-ops)**
- **certifications**
- **handouts**
- **presentations**
- **letters itemizing what you have accomplished**
- **menus**

Remember the Friend

Having a friend there to help you during assembly can be extremely important. Your friend is there to ask the "right" questions and to look at your portfolio from a "different angle." You may find that your friendship will be tested, especially if he or she does his/her job! Your friend's job is of course to ask you the really hard questions that push you to be your best. Your friend is also here to role-play possible answers you may give the interviewer. Don't take things personally; give that friend honest answers even if they are not your best answers. You'll improve through practice.

Once you have organized your work samples you are then ready to develop the support materials that give your portfolio flow.

Step 3 . . . Putting It Together

Now that you have everything gathered, go ahead and put everything that you've prepared into page protectors and into the 3-ring notebook. Organize your information into appropriate tabbed areas. Remember, we've included several documents on the accompanying diskette that can give you a starting point for creating your documents. Refer to Chapter 10, Resource Guide, for a complete listing of all templates.

- Begin with your **work philosophy** and **career goals**
- Put your **résumé** in another page protector behind the work philosophy/goals page.
- Insert **skill sets** if used.
- Insert **letters of recommendation** where appropriate.
- Order your **work samples** and put them into page protectors. You may want to use connected page protectors to keep samples together. Order the work samples with your best examples first.
- Insert copies of **certifications**, **diplomas**, and **degrees**.
- Insert **community service samples**.
- Insert **professional membership** certificates and service samples.
- Insert **academic plan of study** and **faculty/employer bios**.
- Insert **references.**

Step 4 . . . Developing Support Materials

Now that you have the key elements inserted into the portfolio, it's time to create a few support materials.

Statement of Originality and Confidentiality

This one-page sheet should be placed at the beginning of your portfolio. It states that the portfolio is your work and indicates if certain portions of the portfolio should not be copied.

 Template

Use the document on the accompanying diskette to create your own page. (**stmt of originality.doc**)

Work Sample Overview Cards

An work sample overview card is a small card containing a brief summary of the work sample. Use sheets of blank business cards to print information about each work and service sample in your portfolio. Slide one card in the front of each work sample. Each card should include:

- Title.
- Purpose.
- Date developed.
- Names of team members who developed it.
- Demonstrated skills in key word format—use words that are emphasized on your résumé and heading.

Fund-Raising Brochure

Designed and produced brochure for fund-raising marketing piece - raised $125,000
Summer 2000

Skills - Graphic Design, Color Printing, Fund-Raising, Writing

 **Template**

Use the template on the enclosed disk to create your own work sample overview cards. **(Work Sample Overview Cards.doc)**

Allow for Your Style

You are creating a document that represents you and your career to the world. Be sure it feels like you and is a tool that you feel comfortable using. Some people like to make title pages for each section of their portfolios. You can use clipart, photos, and graphics to give the portfolio your own style. Just be sure that the end result looks professional.

General Rules to Follow

- Put all papers in the page protectors using both the front and back.
- Use colored paper to draw attention to special work or service samples.
- Use the same type of paper on your résumé and references (prepare two extra sets of these to hand out during the interview).
- Proof everything at least three times.
- **NEVER USE YOUR ORIGINALS.**

Step 5 . . . Check It Out

We hope this was not an emergency assembly of your portfolio and that you have at least 12 hours to proof and let the portfolio cool. Here are a few items you should check and recheck:

- Read for typos, spelling, grammar, and format. If you are not good at this, have a friend do it.

- Talk through the sections of your portfolio with a friend, thinking about which parts you will elaborate on in an interview.

- When in doubt take it out. . . if you are not sure or not pleased with an item—leave it out.

- If you have assembled this for a particular interview, make sure you have selected work samples that can meet the needs of the organization.

Assembling an On-the-Job Portfolio

When you have a job, your portfolio can help you keep it and get a pay increase or promotion. The overall organization of the portfolio is the same, except that work/service samples are organized in a chronological order, and your professional goals may be organized by your previous year's professional goals and objectives (or the time since your last appraisal.)

- **Check your calendar**—Get in the habit of writing down the start dates, benchmarks, and completion dates of projects. Write down in your calendar any letters of acknowledgment or awards received. Months from now you will have a road map ready to read and secure your documentation for the portfolio.

- **Stop once a month or so and make two lists of what you have accomplished, planned and unplanned**—If you can't do it once a month, then take 30 minutes once every 90 days and think about your career. Make the appointment with yourself right now; map out the appointments and keep them.

- **Set up a file box or file drawer**—At the end of each project make a second copy of it and put it in your file. At the very least, save it on a disk. Remember that setting aside a copy of your work needs to become reflex; it will save you a lot of chasing when you put together your actual portfolio.

- **Review the job description for your position**—As far in advance of the review as possible, you should reread the job description of your position. It is good to strategically consider your level of skill in each of the position statements. Use the job description to guide your quest for work samples and skill set documentation. You may even want to consider seeking out some certifications that will document and help you recover from any deficits.

If you don't have a specific job description for your position (and many people don't), the solution is simple. Write one now. Give a copy of your job description to your supervisor and seek his or her input. It is helpful and strategic to establish the criteria of your position before your review.

- **Review the performance appraisal standards before the actual review**—It seems simple, but be sure you understand the "rules of the game" at the beginning of the performance period. This may or may not be possible. Some organizations have very general standards or criteria. It is especially true in these cases that you develop your career portfolio and utilize it for the review. Now that you know the specifics, keep them in the back of your mind as you make decisions on your work samples and career activities.

- **Concentrate on your skill sets, your work samples, and professional activities**—The other parts of the portfolio, such as your work philosophy, goals, résumé, awards, and certificates, should appear in your portfolio but not be emphasized. The other sections serve as background and quite often are the subtle support you provide to refresh the reviewer's knowledge of you.

- **Write documentation for other people the way you would like to receive it**—Remember the key elements of good documentation: time frame, skills demonstrated, people on the team, attitude of the individual, and what the future projects could be because of this work.

- **Put it all together**—Put together this year's work in a chronological order or into the major areas set up in your job descriptions. Then be sure to explain to the person reviewing you that you have put together a self-review. Set your supervisor up to utilize your career portfolio. Never just walk in the door with your portfolio; it could be perceived as a threat.

Comments from the Frontline - Thoughts on Creating a Portfolio...

Kate was a director of a not-for-profit daycare. She was looking for a position as a director of a different not-for-profit organization. She wanted a higher salary, more benefits, and to be doing more with the planning side of management rather than just day-to-day operations. Kate took several weeks and put together her portfolio. Here are some of Kate's thoughts on the process:

"When putting my thoughts in order to actually begin deciding what goes into my portfolio, I really struggled with what samples I needed. I kept remembering the line in the book that said 'save everything!' So I went into my personnel file at work (since I'm the boss) and copied all my training certificates, letters of thank you, commendations, and recognitions. Then I began putting them into piles of subject matter or categories."

"I matched materials to letters as appropriate, for instance I had received a letter from a conference thanking me for an excellent presentation. I found the corresponding program booklet and looked up my workshop. I highlighted the workshop listing and put a sticky tab thingy on the page as an indicator of where to find the sample. When I actually put it into my portfolio, I put the letter in one page protector and the program in the very next one. When I chose which training certificates to include, I picked out what talents I wanted to highlight."

"I found that I had way too much that I wanted to include in the book. I had to think about what the interview was and tailor the portfolio to the interview. That meant that I had several things in protector sheets that I took out and/or added, depending on where I was going. I included things like workshop outlines/agendas that I had developed, fundraising publication samples. Pictures of myself with others at fundraising events. Etc.."

"I called four people and asked for reference letters. I typed up a reference list with names, addresses, and phone numbers. I added a short note for each person, identifying what they could tell a prospective employer about my expertise, talents and personality. In addition to having this in the notebook, when I got to the interview I gave them a sheet protector that had a list of the references and a copy of all the reference letters."

"Things that I wished I had included or saved include:

- Good copies of my college diplomas
- Copies of grants or other writing samples
- A stronger statement of my goals (I really struggled with creating the right sentences that said what I wanted and in the language that would get me the executive level job I really was seeking

"I found that the portfolio I created was ideally suited for a middle management position. The reason the portfolio worked for the executive level was because it was a new and foreign concept to those who viewed it. I was given a great deal more credit than was truly warranted, I think!"

Comments from Interviewers

"Great! If I had to do this it would have taken me a year to clean out my car and basement!"

"I can't believe that you saved all these things... what made you save these things?"

"This book really showcases your work. This book is an excellent example of your experience and talents."

"I really liked the book."

"Thank you for giving us a bird's eye view of your experience and expertise. It made our decision to hire you so much easier!"

Congratulations –You have a Career Portfolio!

Whew!! Assembly is a lot of work. If you've gotten to this point and have a finished portfolio in hand, congratulate yourself. You've taken a huge step toward understanding yourself and you're ready to take your portfolio to the marketplace. You have taken time to examine your beliefs and goals and had the opportunity to evaluate your work, your skills, your strengths and weaknesses. You've searched through and found the best examples of your work and you now have a tool for tracking your career.

In the next chapter we'll look at how you can adapt your portfolio into an electronic portfolio. If you want to explore the new frontier of Internet websites and find ways to create new opportunities, read on. If you can't wait to learn how to actually use your portfolio in an interview or review, go on to Chapter 8, The Portfolio in Action ... Getting the Job.

Congratulations on your portfolio!

The finished portfolio involves a lot of hard work!

7 THE ELECTRONIC PORTFOLIO

Technology Levels the "Playing" Field

What exactly is an electronic career portfolio? It is a personalized, career-oriented website that you use to get a job or to make your skills known. It can be accessed from the Internet, or you can control access to the portfolio by putting it on a disk or CD-ROM. The electronic career portfolio contains the same information as your "hard copy" portfolio, but it is organized and accessed differently. Consider this. . . one is linear, like a newspaper which is read one page after the other—the hardcopy one; and one is non-linear, or organized in such a way that you can mix up the order and still make sense, like a website—the electronic career portfolio.

Electronic portfolios can be stored on a CD-ROM, zip, or floppy disk

Why Would I Want an Electronic Portfolio?

"It takes long enough to develop a hard copy portfolio, why would I want to spend all my time developing a website to do the same thing?" You're asking the right question. The beauty of the Electronic Portfolio is it's ability to:

- **cluster ideas that are related** — Consider using the same work sample but showing your link in two or more skill sets. For example, you may have a report you generated which demonstrates your leadership ability, technology, and training skills. If you have separate pages for leadership, technology, and training, you can reference the same sample from each page. You are able to dial in the user to the exact parts of the work sample with the electronic portfolio.

- **search by keywords using buttons or frames** — employers like to scan quickly and get a lot of information.

- **add more of yourself** — as your voice or a video clip. Short sound bites allow you to "show yourself in action". Keep in mind that these files can be big and work fine on a CD but may be too big or take too long for access on a web connection.

- **follow-up your interview with support material** — It is appropriate to leave a "copy" of your career portfolio in electronic form for an interviewer to review at a later time.

- **provide new and different work samples that supplement your hard copy portfolio** — You can include more work samples in the electronic portfolio that support your paper portfolio.

So. . . Do I Even Need a Paper Career Portfolio?

Oh, yes! The hardcopy and the electronic portfolio include the same elements, but people process, view, and explore the information differently. The paper (hardcopy) portfolio and the electronic portfolio work differently in the career market.

Hardcopy Portfolios

■ Hard copies work better in interviews. They are more flexible and easier to manage in an interview setting. They allow you to interact with the interviewer in a personal way.

■ Some people may not have access or be comfortable using a computer.

■ It is usually faster to make changes to a hard copy portfolio by switching out work samples to meet the needs of an interview. It takes more time to adjust the contents of an electronic portfolio.

When Does the Electronic Portfolio Become Attractive?

■ Follow up. . . after a successful interview. . . so that others who did not get time to spend with you can be SOLD on you.

■ When they want more time with you after the interview to learn even more about you.

■ It is something they can view without time restrictions.

■ It is a perk that you have some technology literacy.

■ It is a support vehicle—it is not the primary source.

Electronic Portfolios Work Differently

Electronic portfolios are used differently than printed ones—you can't expect the person to whom you are showing it to run and get his/her laptop. You can, however, use it as the copy you leave with the interviewer to support your printed copy. People process information differently, and tabbed work samples and statements support what you say. With the electronic portfolio and the non-linear approach, you can never be sure in what order people will view your info—so it becomes more important that it can stand alone and is organized into chunks.

Wait! - I'm not a "Techno-Wizard"— How Can I Do This?

If you're feeling a little intimidated right now, thinking you don't have the skills or ability to design a website or something really technical… relax. There are several ways to get this accomplished and it doesn't have to cost a lot. You are either going to design this website yourself or you're going to get someone to help you. There are actually many easy-to-use programs for designing websites where you don't have to know any "code" or "HTML" stuff, and some are even free.

Stay focused on your goal. If you have problems "coding" or getting something to work like a graphic or a table or a form, call in your "tech" buddies or friends for help. Don't let the technology manage you. Don't give up. Local universities have plenty of places with lab assistance.

> ## No Coding!!!
>
> **Students! Check your computer lab resources to see what programs are already available! Microsoft FrontPage 2000 is an easy-to-use program for creating web pages. You can also create web pages in Microsoft Publisher and Microsoft Word.**

Getting It All Together

- **What do you already have on disk?** — Find projects, reports, presentations, budgets, etc., that you already have in electronic format.

- **Get the rest of your documents into electronic format —** (Take your tote box to a friend with a scanner!) This can take some time, so allow ½ a day or so for this.

- **Get yourself an electronic suitcase —** Find a way to store all these files. You can put files on several diskettes, a Zip disk, a writable/rewritable CD-ROM disk, or have someone burn a CD-ROM disk for you with all your samples.

- **Get the software you will use to develop the web page and figure out how to use it —** (or get your techno friend to help).

- **Not all work samples belong on your electronic portfolio —** Prioritize and choose your best samples. You may need to customize your electronic portfolio for a potential employer, so scan all of your work samples.

- **Now you're ready to design your site!**

Designing the Electronic Career Portfolio

- Start with a solid working hardcopy career portfolio.

- Consider your style and your "look," including:

    - Fonts.

    - White space.

    - Graphics and photos.

- Decide how you will structure the items to be used including Work Samples, Work Philosophy, Goals, Résumé, References, Certificates, etc. Will they go on separate pages, or will some of them be together?

- Use templates and wizards where possible.

- Choose the work samples—remember than you can organize them in a non-linear way.

- Storyboard the electronic portfolio; that is to say, take a really big sheet of paper and colored markers or pencils and draw pictures of what you want where and what links or references you want on the contained pages. If you have access to a classroom or boardroom, use the chalk or white board. Take a good look here at how much information you want to give in the "big" picture. How much info do you want to have connected and how do you want the people to navigate or move through your portfolio? Consider using basic web HTML editors.

- Design the site on your computer.
- Test it to make sure it works. Pull in a few friends and have them take a look. Revise the site as needed.
- Write the instructions for executing the files. Attach them to the holder of your disk or the cover letter with your website.
- Then go for it—electronically produce the portfolio, date, and make copies. If you have to acquire a new skill, consider how it will support you in your career. In today's world most people are used to navigating a website and understand how they work.

How do I put it on the Internet?

- **Get an ISP – find a spot on the web to "host" your website**
- **Create your web pages on your computer**
- **Upload or FTP the files to the Internet site**

- Find a site to host your page
- Once you've developed a website on your computer you need to get it from your computer to the Internet. Keep in mind that when it's on the Internet, everyone can access it unless you know how to password protect it and so on.

- You need to find a host for your website. There are a lot of free and inexpensive ways. First, check with your Internet service provider (ISP) to see if you can put up a free personal website – many ISPs include a "personal" site as part of your monthly dial-up fee. You can also get space on other sites. Many colleges and universities offer free web space for every student.

Upload Your Files

- Once you've got a place to put your site, you need to "upload" your files from the computer to the web. This process is called FTPing, or publishing your files.

- You will be given a user name and password that will allow you to upload the files to a specific location on the website. To update the site you make changes to the pages on your computer and then upload the files to the web. If you know how to copy and paste files between directories on a computer, you can update your site. If you need assistance, find a friend to help.

Maintaining Your Site

- Put up current work samples as you create them.
- Don't forget to take it down. When you get the job or achieve the goal it may be time to take down your site. You don't want to generate "business" if you're unable to accept it.

 Bright Idea!
Don't forget to include your web address in your hard copy portfolio!

🌱 Ask the Expert - Publicizing my Site

Q. Should I include the web address in my résumé?

A. It depends on how well dialed in you are to this particular employer. It's very tempting on the electronic portfolio to put more there than you need. You still need to strategically design the website to meet the needs of the employer.

Making the Most of Your Electronic Portfolio

In all cases, electronic or paper, the career portfolio is a tool for demonstrating who you are and what knowledge and skills you have—use the portfolio to help people learn about you and your attitude. The mental process of developing a career portfolio is the same for a paper hard copy and an electronic portfolio. The real benefit of the electronic portfolio is the ability to give people more time to access your portfolio. For examples of electronic portfolios visit our website http://learnovation.com.

The following pages show a basic electronic portfolio. This portfolio was designed and created by Karl, an 11-year-old who is currently looking for ways to get money for college. Take this basic idea and expand it to meet your needs.

This site was created with Microsoft FrontPage 2000. You can access this site online at **http://learnovation.com/kportf/index.htm**

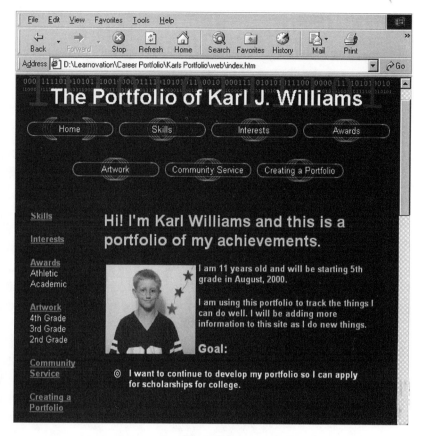

Home Page

The Home page serves as a starting point for the electronic portfolio. It introduces who you are and serves to orient the viewer to your website. Navigation buttons are shown on top, while text navigation is shown on the side. Underlined text are links to additional pages.

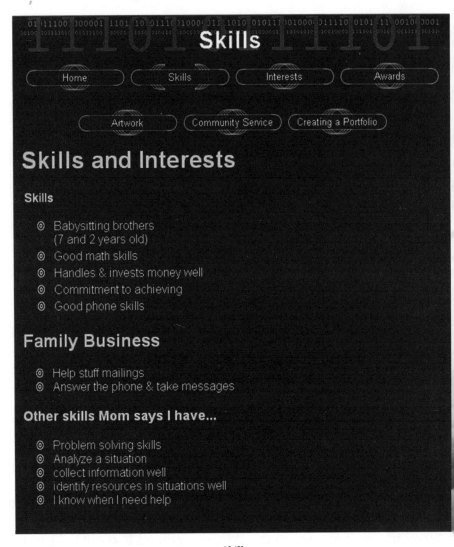

Skills

This page shows specific skills Karl has achieved. As he acquires work samples in these areas, he can create and link to additional pages.

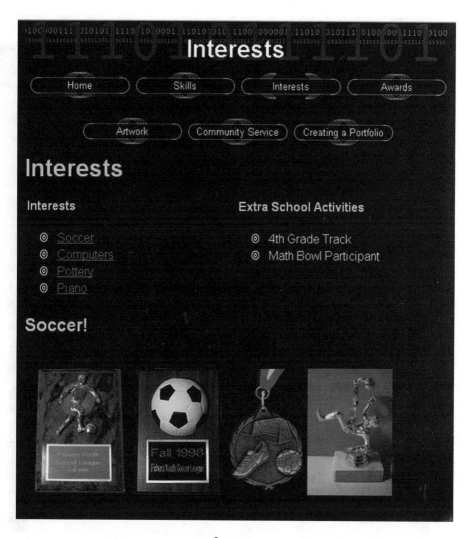

Interests

Karl has grouped all his interests together on one page. He has created internal links on the page, so clicking on a underlined interest takes you to a corresponding location on the page. Users can also scroll down the page.

Karl used a flatbed scanner to import some of the images. For 3-dimensional objects, he used a digital camera and edited them in Photoshop.

Pottery

 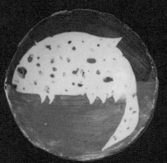 

Computers

I like working with computers. Here is some of the software I have been using:

- ◎ Microsoft Word - Word Processing
- ◎ Dragon System for Teens - Voice Recognition Software
- ◎ Front Page - Web design

I will be taking a one-week class this summer on Digital Cameras and Photoshop!

- ◎ Microsoft Word - Word Processing
- ◎ Dragon System for Teens - Voice Recognition Software
- ◎ Front Page - Web design

I will be taking a one-week class this summer on Digital Cameras and Photoshop!

In 3rd Grade, my Mom and her business partner, Karen, came in and created a website with my class. We had a cool website! - I was on the Design team.

Piano

 I'm just getting started on the piano.

Interests - continued

Awards

Awards - continued

Karl grouped his awards by activity.

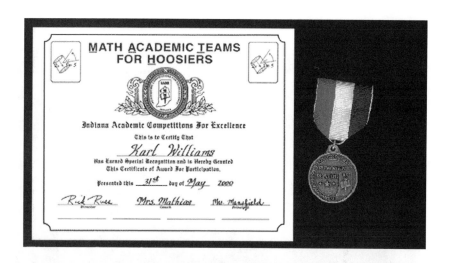

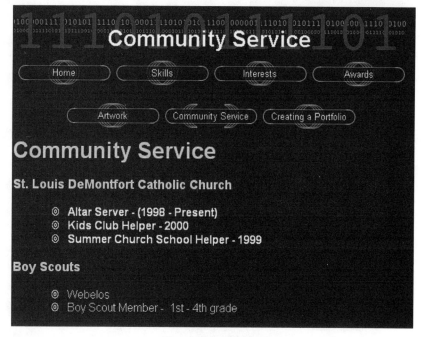

Community Service

Community Service is a great place to include pictures of yourself in action. Karl should add pictures of Boy Scout activities on this page.

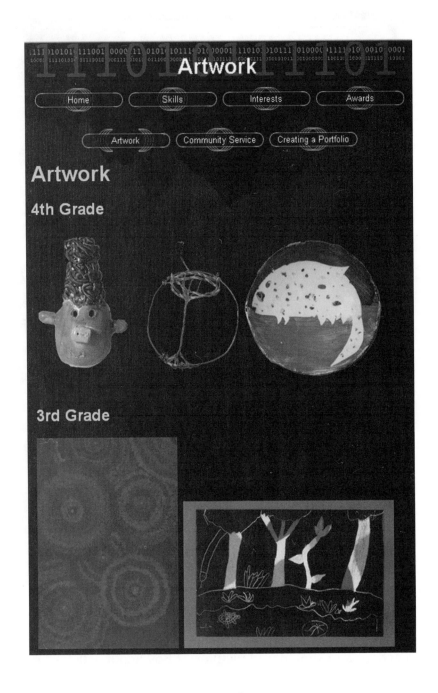

Artwork

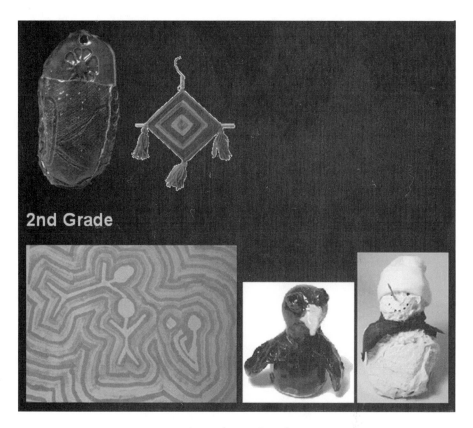

2nd Grade

Artwork - continued

Additional work samples could include reports, project summaries, slides, and presentations. Remember that the web is a more graphic environment. People get bored very easily with loads of heavy text. Use graphics and clipart to make your site more appealing.

3 Using Your Portfolio

Having a completed portfolio is a great achievement. You now have a book that is all about you... your skills, your achievements, your goals and philosophy, your certifications and your résumé. The next step is to customize the portfolio to your needs and to use it as a tool for advancing your career. In this chapter we'll look at specific ways to use your portfolio in a job interview and in a job review or promotion process.

Know Your Portfolio

After all the work of assembling your portfolio, you will have a good idea of your goals, your skills, what you are good at, and the areas where you want to improve. You should also know the contents of your portfolio: your résumé, the work samples for different areas, your certificates, and community service. You want to be able to use your portfolio in an interview without hesitation. Know your goals and work philosophy without having to read them from the page. Remember the different tabbed areas and what samples you have in each.

Good marketing is required of you and your work. Promote your portfolio ahead of time by placing a note at the bottom of your résumé: *Professional Portfolio Available upon Request.* You should also refer to the portfolio in your cover letter when communicating with a company. Your portfolio is one of the prominent tools you take to the interview.

Grab a friend and test drive your portfolio before you need it!

Job Interviews

Match the Portfolio to the Employer

Your portfolio will be most effective and you will be a stronger candidate for the job when you customize your presentation for each employer. Look at the job descriptions and requirements, and use this to target your portfolio. If they want to see management experience, pull together letters and work samples that document your management skills. If you are applying for a position in customer service, show them thank you letters from previous customers and include the certificates you earned at any customer service workshops. As the requirements for the job change, the samples you include in your portfolio should change. You may choose to have a core set of work samples that stay in your portfolio and then add additional samples that may be relevant to the interview. Take time to customize your portfolio before each interview, and your presentation will be much more effective.

Interviewing Tips

During the interview, it's important to let the interviewer know within the first 15 minutes that you have your portfolio available. Remember that the portfolio can be used to introduce you, provide an overview of who you are, or as specific documentation for a question you have been asked. Watch the interviewer for signals of which use will be preferred. He or she may want to see your portfolio right away. You should use it to set up the interviewer to ask you the questions you want to answer and that you can answer best.

Be prepared for a thorough and complete presentation of your portfolio. When using it as an overview, you have the lead in the interview—you can steer the direction of the questions. Take time constraints into consideration. If you have been allotted a 30-minute interview, you should be able to overview your portfolio in five to eight minutes, unless there are questions being asked.

Orient the interviewer to your portfolio

Actually showing the portfolio may seem physically awkward. You may be sitting opposite the person by the time you are ready to show the portfolio. You should get up and stand beside the person to talk briefly through the sections. Make sure your head is not above the interviewer's head. Kneel or bend down to accomplish this. Usually the person viewing it will already be seated. It's difficult to read upside down, so get up and stand next to the person or people interviewing you.(A gentle reminder—women should pay attention to their necklines when leaning over. Both men and women should be sure their deodorant is working!) If it is not feasible to stand next to the interviewer, you can show your portfolio across a desk. Try show it at an angle so you can both see the portfolio.

Here are some guidelines for using your portfolio during the interview:

- **Begin by overviewing your work philosophy and professional goals**—(This shows that you have plans and focus—spend a little time here.)

- **Point out your résumé and remind the person that he or she already has a copy**—(Of course you should have a spare résumé tucked in the inside pocket of the portfolio.)

- **For each additional section, describe briefly what the viewer or reader will find**—Read the work sample overview card on work or service samples. Spend time sharing components of the work or service sample which may not be obvious in your materials. You may have photos with brief captions that need to be expanded upon. You may have sections of projects which need a brief explanation or background. Let the viewer determine how much detail you should go into in each area.

- **Don't use the portfolio to shut off questions from the recruiter**—Give enough overview to peak the person's curiosity so he or she can ask better questions of you. When you're finished showing the portfolio, leave it in front of the person and return to your chair.

What Can Go Wrong? . . .

Be aware of a person's personal space and hold the appropriate distance from the individual. If you approach and the person backs away, you need, as a courtesy, to back off as well. You may turn the pages, or if the person seems to be "in possession" of the portfolio, you can signal him or her to turn the page. Some people will not mind you in their personal space, but be sure to manage any and all of your sexual energy if you are getting close to the person.

Usually what follows, after an overview of the portfolio, are better focused questions from the person interviewing you. Remember, the portfolio is the opportunity you use to present your skills and competencies.

Answering Questions

The interviewer may have some starched predetermined format which he or she believes will not lend itself to looking at your portfolio. Fear not! If within the first five minutes of the interview the person has not expressed an interest in the portfolio, be prepared to use it as a means for answering a specific question about your résumé. It should be easy to answer these questions because you had to answer the same types of questions during the portfolio development process.

Here are some questions that lead themselves to be answered by a look at your portfolio:

- **"What are your five-year goals?"** or **"What are your future plans?"** (See the work philosophy and professional goals section.)

- **"How confident are you on the computer?"** (See the work/ service samples with projects that are computer generated, demonstrating the software and skills they want to see, such as spread sheets, word processing and data base projects or any specialty software.)

- **"What do you do for recreation or release?"** (Show them your community service section.)

- **"What was your most difficult class?"** (Show them a work sample from your class.)

- **"Have you ever . . . ?"** (Fill in the blank and show the person a work or service sample.)

- **What certifications do you hold?** (See the certifications, diplomas, and degrees sections.)

- **"Have you ever worked as part of a team?"** (Show them the work/service samples sections where you have already noted this on your work sample overview card.)

Don't be surprised if the interviewer asks to see the entire portfolio and not just the one section you are showing him or her.

What to Do if They Are Not Interested

You may find that the interviewer has never heard about using a portfolio before. Additionally, he or she may not want to take the time to review it. Some people fear the unknown.

It is possible that a specific question you are asked may be answered best by showing a work sample or other section of your portfolio. In one case, a young man had the portfolio with him and the group leading the interview did not want to see it. However, part way through the interview he used it to answer one question. This went on to spark an interest in the entire portfolio. By the end of the interview, the team of interviewers were fighting to see it before he left the interview. You must be able to clearly explain what a portfolio is and how it works. Don't be surprised if the interviewer tells you he or she has never seen one before.

Normally, you will be able to find some way to work the portfolio into the interview or review. However, if you do not spark the interviewer's interest, even after a clear offering and explanation of what the portfolio is, you may want to consider that you may not be suited for that type of organization

Do I Leave My Portfolio?

What do you do if they want to keep it? It's up to you whether or not you leave your portfolio. If you choose to leave your portfolio, leave it only for a short period of time—24-48 hours. Remember, your portfolio should be a quality copy. At no time should the portfolio have your original copy of anything.

There are advantages and disadvantages to leaving your portfolio with someone. The disadvantage is that they may copy items from it to get ideas to further their business while not specifically following up with getting you hired. On the other hand, if you leave your portfolio, you have created the opportunity to go back and have another contact with the person or company. Before you leave the interview, set a firm time to pick it up. For example, on a Friday noon interview, set the pickup time as Monday noon. Be sure to call and check before picking up the portfolio. You may have peaked their curiosity enough to have them show it to other people. Remember to include the statement of confidentiality in the beginning of your portfolio.

On occasion, human resource people may want to copy your portfolio to include it with your records. You shouldn't hesitate to give permission for your portfolio to be copied, unless you have a proprietary work sample in it. For example, if you have a series of recipes developed for a company that are proprietary, don't give permission for these to be copied. Your exhibit cards should specifically state that this work should not be copied.

After the Interview

Take time after your interview to debrief. Your portfolio may have been a hit, it may have impressed them, it may have intimidated them, or they may have ignored it. Take time after your interview to debrief. Were they interested in your portfolio? Did you feel rushed in presenting it? Did it stay shut in your lap during the whole interview? Think about how you used it and how you can improve. Keep these things in mind for your next interview.

I Blew Them Away...

You may be saying—great. They let me talk about my skills and interests based upon my portfolio. They didn't ask me many questions, or they spent all their time on one section. They just looked at my portfolio. Is that good or bad? Remember to use your portfolio to describe your skills, efforts, and achievements. Be humble and clear with the interviewer. If the interviewer was overwhelmed with who you are, then perhaps you are not well suited for that organization.

It is possible that by using your portfolio, you found out sooner, rather than later, that you are over-qualified for the position. Remember that not everybody is using a portfolio, and those who are may not be using them well. You have stood out among your peers. Some companies will practically make you an offer on the spot; others will see you as a threat. Either way, let the truth prevail. Be yourself, don't try to be someone you are not. Your style, knowledge, skills, and interests will be suited for the right company, and your portfolio is a tool designed to help you find the right match for employment in your industry.

Follow-Up

Be sure to followup with a thank you letter to the interviewer. Thank you letters should be relatively brief, thanking the interviewer for his or her time. Try to include some personal comment that will help the interviewer remember you. Comments about your portfolio may help jog their memory.

Joe's "Rejection" Letter...

Can't see the point of a thank you letter for a rejection? Joe had an interview for a position on Tuesday. He had been specifically asked to apply for the position and thought the interview had gone well. He was angry and upset when he received a rejection letter in the mail on Wednesday. Nevertheless, he sent a thank you letter, indicating that it was good to meet the interviewer and he hoped she would keep him in mind for positions in the future. The next day he received a frantic phone call from the interviewer. She told him his résumé had gotten into the wrong pile! He never should have received the letter, and he was most definitely being considered.

Thank you's create good will and extend your presence to the interviewer. You never know when this may come back to you.

Using the Portfolio at a Job Review

When you are hunting for a job, you are using your portfolio to convince people that you are worth the time and effort of hiring and training for a position. You have to show them why you will fit with the company and how you can contribute. Now that you have the job, you need to show them what you can do and why you should be a valued employee.

A New Focus

As you work through this book you are creating a "career" portfolio, not a "job-hunting" portfolio. While searching for a job, your portfolio represents a wide range of samples, showing what you can do. Once you have a job, the focus of your portfolio shifts to a "promotion/review" portfolio, where you track your performance and achievements on the job. Now the focus is on setting quarterly and yearly goals and recording and demonstrating your accomplishments. You will still be collecting work samples, tracking committee involvement, documenting special projects and accommodations, and tracking certifications and seminars you have attended, etc. Your goal is to prove your worth and win a raise or promotion.

Mapping to Annual Goals

Your career portfolio is an ideal place to keep track of your goals and objectives. Make a list of your goals at the beginning of each quarter or for your quarterly review. You may want to make a checklist where you check off items as they are completed. You could also create your own skill sets for any areas in which you want to demonstrate your ability. If one of your goals is to improve your computer skills, you could create a computer skills list and check off on your level of ability. You would also include any certificates from computer courses sponsored by the company or those you pursued on your personal time. Include professional development goals as well. Talk with your supervisor and discuss your ideas for tracking your performance. He or she may be delighted to use it as a review tool and they may even decide that the rest of the department should create portfolios!

Unplanned Accomplishments

Use your portfolio to track things you have done that weren't on your list of quarterly goals. Take time as you do projects, and work with people to write down what you have done so you can include it in the portfolio. If you have bailed out a co-worker on a deadline or taken over additional responsibilities for someone on maternity leave, document these activities. This can show your boss that you are a team player and you can pitch in as needed. If you volunteered to write instructions for a module or you lead the company volleyball team to the league championships, don't forget to include a picture and brag a little! You should also include any volunteer work or community service efforts— employers love to see this! If you served as the United Way chairperson and motivated your co-workers to give the highest amount in five years, make a note of it in your portfolio.

Working with the Boss for the Review

When you are nearing your review, let your boss know that you have a portfolio and have been using it to track your performance. Let him or her know several days in advance of the review. Offer to show it beforehand, so he or she has an idea of what you have been up to. Keep your résumé up-to-date and current. Be sure to explain to your boss that your résumé is there to summarize your work history and experience, not because you are looking for another job!

You will use your portfolio to summarize and review your work. The actual techniques of talking the reviewer through the content is the same for the performance review as it is for the interview. Use it to overview your work and performance or use it as a reply to a question. Remember that your career portfolio is a living document and changes as you do.

The first time you present your portfolio, be prepared for the reviewer to show some uncertainty since it may be a very new concept to the person. Also be prepared to go through two reviews. One will be at the 5-10 minutes where you mini-present your portfolio prior to the formal review. During this session you will explain the organization of your work and how to read your portfolio. Set your supervisor up to utilize your career portfolio. Never just walk in the door with your portfolio.

There are several effective ways to use the portfolio during the actual full review. Consider using it as a way to present your own self-appraisal. Another possible technique is to use it to answer specific questions about your performance patterns. Yet another way is to use it as a summary tool at the end of the formal process. The key to making the portfolio work is to allow the reviewer enough time with your career portfolio to use it as a guide. Several industries and organizations have found that performance portfolios have been healthy additions to their personnel review process. This is especially true in the hospitality industry and in the computer technology training field, but it is a growing process in most professional fields. Everyone wants proof these days.

Using the Portfolio to Get a Promotion

Now that you know how to use the portfolio during your performance review, let's talk about how to use it during the reviews where you are up for a promotion. Promotions can be new titles, new assignment to a different branch of the organization, or simply progression within the company hierarchy. In any of these cases, your portfolio should reflect your work from the period of your last promotion. If that was two years ago, then your work should reflect the last two years. If you have not been promoted yet, have your portfolio reflect your work from the time you began your employment.

Work samples, should be just that—samples... don't include everything you have done. Just as in the career portfolio, you need to choose highlights of your best work. Even if something is not able to fit on an 8.5" x 11" sheet of paper you should still include it. You might want to include a summary sheet in your portfolio and indicate that the full project is available for review. Your choices should summarize as many skills as possible and as much professional growth as possible. In these cases it may be appropriate to include prior good reviews as evidence of your wonderful performance, which is, of course, deserving of the reward of a pay increase and/or the "corner office."

The key to your success is to let the person reviewing you know why you have a portfolio:

Reason #1—This is how you keep track of your own professional development.

Reason #2—This is designed to save time and assist your reviewer in the process.

Reason #3—It is a tool to help you in the review process.

Be prepared to teach your reviewer how to use your portfolio. Your employer may want to compare you to others in the organization. All these elements and issues can serve you well as you grow and progress as a professional in your field. Don't ever apologize for work you are proud of having done. A portfolio is a great way to break out the different aspects of your career. If you do have an area which needs development then at least your achievements will get some attention as well. Remember the portfolio is a reflection of you—make the most of it.

9 A Matter of Style

You are a professional, you have the credentials and the confidence to get ahead. You need to make sure your portfolio projects the same impression. If your portfolio looks sloppy and disorganized, don't even bother to take it to the interview or meeting. Your portfolio must look as clean, organized, and professional as you do.

The focus of this section is on style: the look, feel, and presentation of the materials in the portfolio. This section provides some basic guidelines for producing your work samples and other documents in your portfolio by taking a look at:

- Working with words and pictures (text and graphics).
- Production tips for video and photography.
- Physical production of materials using copiers, scanners, and printers.

Text

Have you ever been reading something and suddenly you realize that you have no idea what you just read for the last four pages? This happens to all of us, but why? Are we not concentrating hard enough, or is the material boring? Your goal in creating your career portfolio is to keep the person reading it awake and interested. You need to make sure that the information is easy to understand, well organized, and presented in an interesting style. You want the reader to grasp the meaning of your work without needing to read every word.

Some people write the way they talk—you can almost hear their voices. Your writing needs to have a "voice" when people read it; otherwise everything becomes just words on paper. Be yourself. Your goal is to say what you need to in your professional voice, in a clear, clean, and concise way.

Just as important as the words you use is the look and feel of the text. The following section will give you ideas for improving the style of your words.

- **Organize first** — Decide what you want to say before you begin writing.

- **Create an outline** — Outline the main ideas of what you want to say; then go into detail in each idea.

- **Use "mind-mapping"**—Mind mapping is the process of writing ideas on paper, grouping words and ideas, and clustering ideas in a non-linear format.

- **Compose at the computer** — Today, many people compose and write at the computer, since they can keyboard information faster than they can write it down on paper.

- **Have a friend take notes** — Talk to someone else and have them jot down notes. This is a great way to start getting organized.

- **Use a conversational tone** — Use a relaxed and informal style of writing. Write in first person, using I, as in I have done this..., I participated in..., I am managing....

- **Use active vocabulary versus passive** — Active vocabulary projects the idea that you are currently working on something. Compare the use of passive words such as **does, get, show**, to active words like **doing, getting, showing**.

- **Avoid slang and too much jargon** — While it may look impressive, colloquialisms may turn what you are saying into code. Remember, the goal is to make everything clear and easy to understand.

- **Tell the truth** — It's always easier to write what you believe and what you have done versus making things up and trying to be impressive.

- **Proof your work**—Proofing your work ensures a professional look and feel to the documents you produce. Spelling, punctuation, or grammar errors can be embarrassing.

- **Use bullet points**—Bullets are an easy way to organize information in a readable, concise way. You've probably noticed after reading through this book that we, the authors, love to use bullet points. Here's a bulleted list, listing some of the reasons to use bullet points:

  - Bullets let you highlight key points in the text.

  - Bullets make it easier for a reader to quickly scan through information.

  - Bullets are often used when you are listing several points or examples.

  - Using bullets can eliminate unnecessary text from sentences.

Now, take a look at the same information, written in paragraph form rather than using bullets, and decide which is easier to read:

> Bullets pull out key information and make it easier for a reader to quickly scan through a lot of information. Bullets are often used when you are listing several points or examples. They also can eliminate unnecessary text from sentences.

Elements of Text

- **Fonts.**
- **Margins, tabs, and spacing.**
- **White space.**

Text Areas of the Portfolio:

- **Management Philosophy.**
- **Goals.**
- **Résumé.**
- **Work samples.**

- **Community Service.**
- **References.**
- **Professional memberships and services.**
- **Work sample overview cards.**
- **Labels for photos and video.**

Fonts

The look and style of the letters in your documents come from the fonts. Fonts are one of the simplest ways to control the look of your document, and can be used to let your creativity and personality flow onto the page.

Serif vs. sans serif fonts—There are thousands of fonts available these days. All of these fonts fall into two major categories: Serif or Sans Serif. Each of these groups has a different look and can be used to emphasize specific pieces of information in the document.

Serif fonts have the little flourishes at the ends of letters. The font you are reading now is a serif font called Friz Quadrata. Notice the curve of an "a" or the edges on a "T."

Examples of serif fonts are:

Times New Roman   Garamond   Bookman Old Style

Sans serif fonts don't have the flourishes and curves in the letters.

Examples of sans serif fonts are:

Arial   Humanist   Dom Casual   Tahoma

Decorative Fonts — Be careful when you use decorative and funky fonts. These can be serif or sans serif. They are great for projects and section pages in your portfolio, but don't use them as main text in a document. They are hard to read. Use them as accent only, and never on a résumé. Examples of decorative fonts include:

Marydale   Party   Burweed ICG   Gurnsey

Guidelines for Font Usage

There are no strict rules for the use of fonts, but here are some general guidelines:

- **Use serif fonts for body text**—Serif fonts are easier to read because our eyes use the little flourishes on letters to distinguish the letters. Most of the books you read are in a serif typestyle.

- **Use sans serif fonts for headings**—Sans serif fonts are often used for headings and titles rather than text. They are used to capture interest and draw attention to a particular section.

- **USE ALL CAPS SPARINGLY— USING ALL CAPITALS CAN BE DISTRACTING AND HARD TO READ. THE USE OF ALL CAPS ON THE WEB OR IN AN E-MAIL IS THE EQUIVALENT OF SHOUTING.**

- **Don't be afraid to experiment with different fonts**—Find one that says something about your personality, be it *elegant,* **bold,** stylish, or **slightly wild.** Just remember, it must be readable. You don't want your reader struggling to see what the text says. If text is hard to read, we usually stop reading and skip to something else, which could cause someone to bypass some very important information about you. Consider using this type of font in the title or heading section.

- **Don't mix too** *many* **fonts together** *in* **a document** — Try to stick to one font for text and another for headings. Your work can look jumbled if you use too many variations.

- **Bold and italic** — The same goes for bold and italic: Use them sparingly, when you need something emphasized.

- **Avoid underlining text!** — <u>Underlining is a tool that was used in the era of the typewriter, when we didn't have bold and italic.</u> **Don't use it.**

- **Use a proportional font** — Speaking of typewriters, have you ever noticed how every letter on a typewritten document takes up the same amount of space? Proportional fonts will take up less space, let you fit more on a page, and are easier to read. In the sample on the next page, both paragraphs are set in 12 point size, but the non-proportional looks bigger:

```
This text is an example of a non-proportional
font. Every character or space takes up the
same amount of space.(Courier)
```

This text is an example of a proportional font. Each character takes up as much room as it needs. (Friz Quadrata)

- **Leave only one space after a period** — Remember the typing rule about leaving two spaces after a period? Two spaces were used so you could easily see the end of a sentence in the typewriter age. With the advent of word processors and proportional fonts, we don't need the extra space. You may think it's a hard habit to break, but it is actually very easy to do.

- **Choose the correct font sizes** — The size of the font also affects the readability of the document. The most common size is 12 point. This book is written in 12 point font to make it easy to read at a glance. 10 point is the smallest size we recommend using on résumés and other documents. Any smaller, and it is very hard to read. The text in footers and headers can be smaller than 10 point, as long as they are still readable.

- **Watch the size of headings** — Most headings are printed in 16 to 18 point. Make sure your heading isn't too big for the text; meaning, don't combine 18 point headings with 10 point text.

- **Use spell checking** — All good word processors contain a program to check spelling. Use this to correct typing and spelling mistakes. OK, this is an obvious step, but it's amazing how many documents we see where this simple, convenient step was overlooked. Typos look bad (especially on the front page of your portfolio!).

- **Don't rely on the spell checker** — Proof your work. Too many people rely on the spell checker to catch all their mistakes. Unfortunately the spell checker can't recognize words that are spelled correctly but misused in a sentence.

(You no that I'm talking about, don't ewe?— You **know w**hat I'm talking about, don't **you**?)

- **Single space your text** — You're probably familiar with single and double spacing. Double spacing is commonly used for reports, but single spacing should be used for most of the documents in your portfolio. Generally, you leave a double space between headings and the body of the text.

- **Use customized line spacing** — If you "get into" designing the look of your documents, you may discover that a double space after a heading is too much space. If you really want to customize your document, play with settings for the space above or below the text. This command is often found in the same location as the single or double spacing commands, and can be used to add extra spacing before or after a heading.

Which of the following combinations looks best to you?

Work Philosophy: *(single spaced)*

I believe that every person should receive excellent customer service.

Work Philosophy: *(double spaced)*

I believe that every person should receive excellent customer service.

Work Philosophy: *(6 points)*

I believe that every person should receive excellent customer service.

Margins, Tabs, and Spacing

The margins, tabs, and spacing you use in a document will change depending on what you are producing. Keep in mind how the document will be used when setting up the page.

Here are some general rules:

- **Use a generous margin around the page** — Allow a generous margin around your page, generally 3/4" to 1" around the entire page. Don't make your margins any smaller than 1/2", or your page will look crowded. Many people like to make notes in the margins of a résumé during an interview, and good use of white space in the form of margins allows this. Wider margins also give documents a clean and open look.

- **Don't be afraid to go to a second page** — Two or three balanced, open pages look much better than one cramped page. Keep in mind that the information in your documents should be important. Don't go to two pages when you can trim out unnecessary details.

- **Get to know your word processor** — Look for the easy ways to center and indent information.

- **Keep the style consistent** — Decide on a look and style for your portfolio documents, and then stick with it. Use the same margins, fonts, and spacing on these documents.

Headers and Footers

Headers and **footers** are areas of text that appear at the top and bottom of a page, outside the normal space used to enter information. Headers and footers are used to print text that should appear on each page of a document, such as page numbers, dates, titles, or names. In this book, the page numbers and the chapter title appear in the footer. If you are planning to duplex a document (print on both sides of a page), you should use the **mirror margin** settings to have information in your headers and/or footers appear on the opposite sides of a left- and right-facing page.

Header and footer information is entered separately from regular text, and usually has tab settings preset to print information left-justified, centered, or right-justified on the page.

Text placed in a header or footer should be in a smaller font, usually 7 to 9 point. You may want to print a line between the header or footer and the main body of text to keep them separated.

Here's an example of a page with footers:

> **Heading**
>
> a;sdlkfjaslfasd;lfkasjd;a;
> a;akdjflakd;falksdlsklds
> a;lskfjakjadlksjdaiejle;liej
> a;lsdifasifaslfeifalea;sfehi
> a;ldkfafeias;fiefnefiefnlis
> a;lfiealisejlaieja fie efeifflie
> ;lkjlkjlsdfjaieja;lifjaelieff;
> aife iefeif ejfiaef;alsife iefj
> ;alkjlakaieaslifefisefie asie
> a;lkfjaslf slfkjsfljs ssl sf; slf
> ;lkjaliefj idfjle;slfekajsd;flkja
>
> Michael Heroux   Feasibility Study
> Pg. 10   4/26/00

- **Include your name and the page number on each page** — If your document is two or more pages long, include your name and a page number in the header or footer of each page.

White Space

You'll hear graphic designers and desktop publishers constantly babbling about the correct use of white space. No, white space isn't the inside of a padded cell or blizzard conditions in the Midwest; rather, white space is the unprintable area that appears in and around the text and graphics on a page.

When you make the margins wider in a document, you are increasing the amount of white space on the page. Take a look at some of the computer manuals and documentation you've got lying around, and you'll see lots of variations on the use of white space. A page which has narrow margins and lots of text can be tiring to read. A page with too much white space can make a reader think he or she is missing information. When possible, add graphics and pictures to a page to add interest and give the reader's eyes a break.

Here are some examples showing the use of white space on the page:

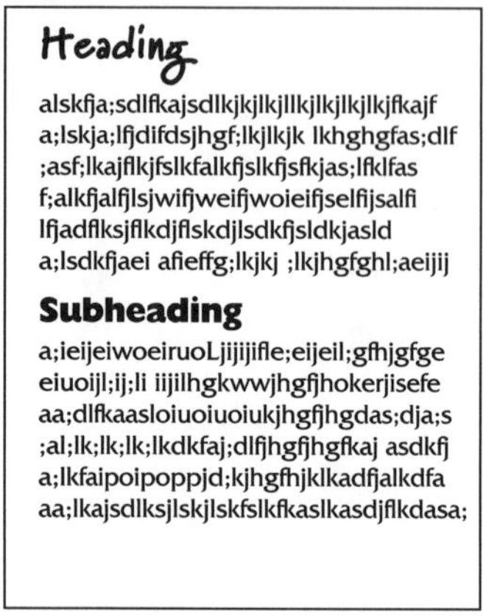

Figure #1

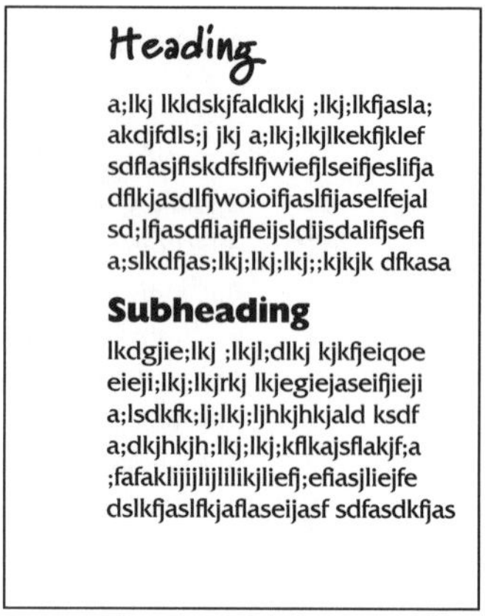

Figure #2

Figure #1 contains very little white space and looks cramped. Compare it to Figure #2 where we added a wide left margin.

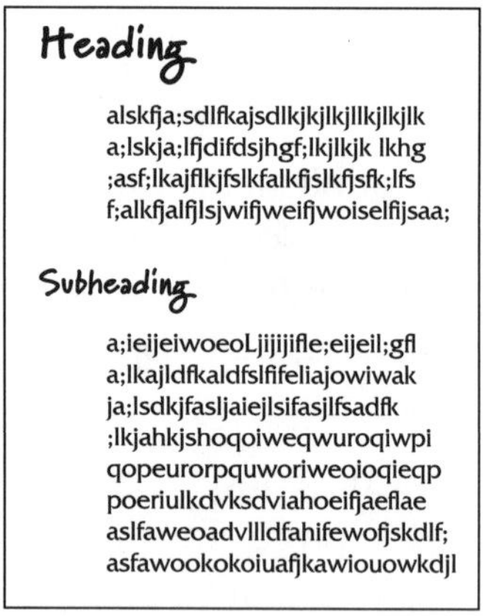

Figure #3

Figure #3 adds side headings to the text to make the headings stand out.

<table>
<tr><td>

Heading

alskfja;sdlfkajsdlkjkjlkjllkjlkjlkjl
a;lskja;lfjdifdsjhgf;lkjlkjk gfas;dl
;asf;lkajflkjfslkfalslkfjsfkjas;lfklfa
f;alkfjalfjlsjwifjwjwoieifjselfijsalfi
lfjadflksjflkdjflsjlsdkfjsldkjasld
a;lsdkfjaei afieffkj ;lkjhgfghl;aeij

Subheading

a;ieijeiwoeiruoifle;eijeil;gfhjgfge

</td><td>

Heading

a;lkj lkldskjfaldkkj ;lkj;lkfjas
akdjfdls;j jkj a;lkj;lkjlkejklef
sdflasjflskdfslfjwilseifjeslifja
dflkjasdlfjwoioiflfijaselfejal
sd;lfjasdflik kkfjsl ljsdifjsefi
a;slkdfjas;lkj;lkj;lkj;;kjkjk dsa

Subheading

lkdgjie;lkj ;lkjl;dlkj kjkfje
eieji;lkj;lkjrkj lkjegie kjkjeji
a;lsdkfk;lj;lkj;ljhkjhkjalddf
a;dkjhkjh;lkj;lkj;kflkajkjf;a
;fafaklijiljlijlilikjlief;esjliejfe
dslkfjaslfkjaflaseijasf sdsdkfjas

</td></tr>
</table>

Figure #4   **Figure #5**

Placement of graphics is another important consideration in the use of white space. Keep pictures aligned with text if possible as in Figure 4. You can also add interest to a page by adding accent lines as in Figure 5.

Visual Media —Working with Pictures and Video

A picture is worth a thousand words. . . If so, it's really important to get your pictures to look their best in order to convey the right impression. There's no question that we learn more quickly from pictures than from words on a page. Like anything else in your portfolio, pictures and videos should demonstrate your ability to perform a specific skill or competency and should be used when words won't convey this or would take too long.

Photographs

Photographs are used to emphasize your work. Take the best shots that demonstrate your work, but don't include too many photos. Photographs can be useful when you want to:

- **Display a finished product** — elegantly decorated cakes, displays, or booths you have created.

- **Put your talents on display** — public speaking, training sessions, anywhere you are in action.

Tips for Taking Better Photographs:

- **You should appear in the photo when possible** — This provides proof that it's your work, not someone else's.

- **Pay attention to film speed** — 100 speed film is good for outdoor shots where you don't need a flash. When shooting indoors, use 200 or 400 speed film, and use a flash.

- **Get close** — Get close to your subject (unless you're photographing wild animals!). Use telephoto shots to get closer if needed.

- **Fill the field** — Use the field finder on the camera and completely fill the picture with the product. Again, get close to the subject!

- **Watch where you stand** — Don't shoot pictures into light. The light meter of a camera adjusts for the brightest light, often making the real subject of the picture too dark.

- **Watch your background** — Most people look a little strange with a flower arrangement for a hat or a pole growing out of their head!

- **Be prepared** — Try out the equipment before you have to take the picture (i.e., know how the equipment works before a critical moment, so you don't forget to take off the lens cap or find out you have dead batteries in your flash!)

- **Use a tripod** — Tripods keep your work steady and prevent blurry pictures.

- **Consider getting a special camera holder** — If you will be taking lots of still shots of products sitting on a table, make a $35 investment in a camera holder specifically designed for taking overhead pictures.

Using Video

Video can be used when you want to show examples of yourself in action. Video takes pictures and adds sound. Keep in mind that no one really enjoys watching home videos, so keep your video short, to the point, and make it worth watching. Limit your video to 3-, 5-, 10-, or 20-minute segments. No one is going to sit through more than a 20-minute video.

Tips for Better Videos:

- **Tips for photos also apply to video.**
- **Emphasize your skills** — Keep the emphasis of your video on your skills, not on your production abilities.
- **Be prepared** — Always test out equipment ahead of time, especially if you are borrowing the equipment. It's always good to have extra batteries and an extension cord handy.
- **Watch your lighting** — Make sure the lighting is correct.
- **Label the video** — Indicate the subject and the length of video clips.

Tips for Looking Your Best in Front of a Lens:
Your looks:

- **Get a good night's rest** — Weariness and stress are visible. Makeup can only cover so much.
- **Make sure your hair looks neat and attractive** — If you need it cut, do it several days in advance.
- **Gentlemen, be careful shaving, avoid scrapes and cuts** — Watch out for "five o'clock" shadow.

- **Women** — wear make up as usual. If you wear heavy liner on your lower eye lid—go lightly or avoid it so that you do not look like a raccoon.

Clothing choices:

- **Wear a proper fitting suit and shirt.**
- **Turtlenecks often make people look** — like turtles in two dimensions.
- **Darker tones make the body look thinner.**
- **Avoid Navy blue** — It shows everything and appears murky.
- **Avoid wearing black and white in color photos.**
- **Avoid wearing white shirts if possible** — it can produce a glare.
- **Wear a suit jacket for a serious look** — Button the top button on all double-breasted suits.
- **Make sure your clothes are not too tight** — If you have recently gained weight, a new larger shirt will mask the gain better than a tight-fitting outfit.
- **Ties should not be remarkably distinctive unless it is a signature look.**
- **Keep your jewelry to a minimum.**

Production Tools—Copiers, Scanners, and Printers

Copiers, scanners and printers are the most common tools you'll use to produce your portfolio. Here are some tips for making their output look as good as possible:

Copiers

- **Clean the machine** —Take a bottle of glass cleaner and a cloth with you the next time you go to make copies. Clean the glass on the machine and you'll find that your final copies will be much clearer.

- **Align the paper** — Center the page on the copier, and make sure the paper is straight on the copier. Nothing is more annoying than crooked copies!

- **Enlarge small fonts** — If the original document is in 10 point or smaller type, you must enlarge it to make it easier to read.

- **Copying small pieces of paper** — If you're copying something smaller than 8.5" by 11", be sure to put a white piece of paper behind the document so the background is clear. If necessary, tape the original to the paper to hold it centered. If you are trimming the copy from a larger size, be sure to use scissors. Think neat.

- **Color copying** — Color copying is expensive. Look at the project and determine if you really need color in your work sample. Use color copying when you want to accent something special.

- **Consider scanning as an alternative** — It's hard to copy photographs, except black and white. You should scan color pictures for higher quality.

- **When in doubt, ask for professional help** — The staff at copy centers are usually happy to assist you with your copying.

Scanning Equipment

- **Scanning is often a good alternative to photocopying** — it can produce a clearer picture. Combined with a color printer, it can also be a cheap alternative to color copying.

- **Resolution** — Scanning is measured in dpi—dots per inch. The higher the dpi, the more detailed and sharper the picture. Use no less than 300 dpi, preferably 600 dpi or higher when scanning.

- **Flatbed scanners vs. hand scanners** — Flatbed scanners allow you to copy larger areas of information at a time, and provide better quality than hand scanners. They provide higher resolution and less hassle.

- **Scan certificates and degrees** — For a better look, consider scanning certificates and degrees; they copy official seals better than a copier.

Paper and Printing

Paper

As you choose the paper you'll use in your portfolio, keep in mind that the main purpose of the paper is to enhance the text and graphics in the document, making it easier to read. It can also be used to distinguish you from other people and can capture a bit of your style. Here are some guidelines for selecting paper:

- **Use high quality, 24 lb. paper** — Heavier weight paper has a better feel and look. It also helps keep printing from showing through to the other side.

- **Don't use fax paper or any type of thermal paper** — Thermal paper will fade and age. Make copies of any faxes.

- **Paper color** — Use subtle colors, nothing harsh. Use the same paper consistently throughout the portfolio. Use color to draw attention to items you want to emphasize or to title pages. Don't overuse colored paper; limit yourself to a maximium of three different colors. White should be your primary color. Make sure your résumé is printed on white paper.

Printing

- **Use a high quality printer** — Good printers can produce 300 to 600 dpi (dots per inch) resolution. The higher the dpi, the higher the quality of the document.

- **Working with inkjet printers** — If you are printing on an ink jet printer, use paper that's been designed for ink jets, or paper that says it's compatible. Ink jet paper is designed to absorb the ink and give you a clearer, sharper image than regular laser jet paper.

- **Color printing** — Use color printing sparingly to accent important information.

- **Don't use dot-matrix printers.**

Tabs and Cards

Here are some ideas to keep in mind when creating the tabs and work sample overview cards used in the portfolio:

- **Buy standard size products** — Avery brand labels are the most popular brand of labels. Most word processors can automatically set up a document based on common sizes of Avery brand labels. If you buy another brand of labels, be sure they have the same label measurements as the Avery brand. Most word processing packages have pre-set templates which lay out the page's margins and space. Setting up labels can be as simple as entering a number off the box. Check out the supply list in Chapter 10, Resource Guide, for specific product numbers.

- **Watch the product's box to see if it is designed for laser or inkjet printers** — If you are printing on an inkjet printer, get the product designed for the inkjet. It is usually brighter and has a coating designed to hold the ink and dry very fast. The ink may spread on products designed for the laser printer. In general, laser and inkjet products are interchangeable, but don't go to all that work and find out the end product looks sloppy.

Follow the guidlines in this chapter and you're sure to have a fantastic looking portfolio! Putting the effort into making your portfolio look professional will pay off in your interviews and reflect the quality back onto you.

Send Us Your Success Story

Our research continues. We are interested in your stories about using the portfolio. We want to hear your experiences and opinions. Tell us how your friends and family reacted. Let us know what you did to improve the portfolio's layout or contents. Share with us how you used the portfolio with your employer and how your organization reacted.

We are interested in the types of work samples you used and how you produced quality copies.Tell us what you would like to see developed or improved in the portfolio. Our next book will expand on the electronic portfolio. If you have any questions, ideas, or comments we would love to hear them. Let us know how we can help.

Please send your success story to:

Learnovation® LLC
My Portfolio
10831 Thistle Ridge
Fishers, IN 46038-2254

or E-mail us at: **portfolio@learnovation.com**

Visit our web page to learn more about career mechanics and other people's portfolio experiences.

http://learnovation.com

10 RESOURCE GUIDE

This resource guide contains the following materials designed to help you make the development of your career portfolio easier:

1. **Supply List** - Materials to purchase

2. **Emergency Instructions for Portfolio Assembly** - When you need to put together a portfolio fast...

3. **Action Verbs** - A list of verbs used when describing what you have done. Typically used on your résumé and in goal-setting.

4. **Department of Labor SCANS** - A listing of general skills and competencies. Useful when setting up skill sets and looking up résumé language.

5. **Templates on Diskette** - A listing of the files included on the diskette which accompanies this book.

1. Supply List

Take this list with you to the office supply store. You can also find these items on the Internet at **http://www.officemax.com** or **http://www.officedepot.com** or **http://www.staples.com**

- **Plastic file tote box** (1)
- **Hanging file folders, standard file size** (20-30)
- **Zippered, 3-ring notebook** (Preferrably leather or simulated leather)
- **Clear sheet protectors** (50-100) Different weights are available:

  Avery 74130 - Diamond Clear© Sheet Protectors - Super Heavy-weight, Top Loading - 50 sheets per box.

  Avery 75530 - Diamond Clear© Sheet Protectors - Standard Weight, Top Loading - 25 sheets per package.

  Avery 74097 - Diamond Clear© Sheet Protectors - Economy Weight, Top Loading - 75 sheets per package.

- **Connected sheet protectors** (3-5 sets)

  Avery 74301 - Bound Sheet Protector Sets - Clear, 10-page set

  Avery 74300 - Bound Sheet Protector Sets - Clear, 5-page set

- **Multi-capacity sheet protectors** — If you want to include a magazine or a project that you would pull out of the sheet protector to view, you can purchase multi-capacity sheet protectors which can hold 50 pages in each protector.

  Avery 74171 - Multi-Capacity Sheet Protectors - 25 sheets per pkg.

  Avery 74172 - Multi-Capacity Sheet Protectors - 10 sheets perpkg.

- **Extra-wide 3-ring tabs with labels** (1-2 sets)

  Tabbed sheet protectors - you can insert a title page into each tabbed page:

  Avery 74160 - Protect 'N Tab ™ Tabbed Sheet Protectors - Clear 5-Tab, Single Set

  Avery 74110 - Protect 'N Tab ™ Tabbed Sheet Protectors - Clear 8-Tab, Single Set

Extra-wide paper dividers:

Avery 11221 - Worksaver® Extra WideTM BIG TAB Insertable Tab Dividers - Laser/Ink Jet, 5-Tab Clear, 3-hole punched

Avery 11222 - Worksaver® Extra WideTM BIG TAB Insertable Tab Dividers - Laser/Ink Jet, 8-Tab Multicolor, 3-hole punched

Avery 11223 - Worksaver® Extra WideTM BIG TAB Insertable Tab Dividers - Laser/Ink Jet, 8-Tab Clear, 3-hole punched

Avery 11220 - Worksaver® Extra WideTM BIG TAB Insertable Tab Dividers - Laser/Ink Jet, 5-Tab Multicolor, 3-hole punched

- **Blank sheets of business cards** (10 sheets)

  Avery 08371 - Ink Jet Business Cards - White, 10 cards per sheet

  Avery 08471 - Ink Jet Business Cards - White, 10 cards per sheet

  Avery 05911 - Laser Business Cards - White, 10 cards per sheet

- **8-1/2" x 11" plastic photo sheet holders** (2-3 as needed)

  Avery 13403 - Photo Pages - Eight 3-1/2" x 5" photos per page

  Avery 13407 - Photo Pages - Four 3-1/2" x 5" horizontal photos per page

  Avery 13406 - Photo Pages - Four 4" x 6" horizontal photos per page

  Avery 13401 - Photo Pages - Six 4" x 6" photos per page

- **Name plate or vinyl card holder**

  Avery 73720 - Self-Adhesive Business Card Holders - for 3-1/2" x 2" business cards, Clear For Inkjet printing: use 24# bright white paper

- **Paper (high quality)**

  Clear For Inkjet printing: use 24# bright white paper

2. Emergency Portfolio Instructions

I Need a Portfolio Now!!!

"Oh, it won't take that long to put it together."

"I have one that I used last time."

"My interview is tomorrow and I have to do all this before I can start on my portfolio?"

"Do I update my portfolio, or do I sleep and shower?"

If you've just purchased this book and want to put together a portfolio for an interview tomorrow morning, or if you've had this book for a while and suddenly your interview is upon you, there's still hope. Based on several frantic experiences of our own, rest assured you can put together a basic career portfolio in three hours if you have a computer, printer, and your best friend's help.

Run to the Office Supply Store and Buy:

- **Zippered, 3-ring binder**
- **Clear page protectors (a box or two of 50)**
- **Extra-wide page tabs**
- **Plastic stick-on business card holder for front of portfolio**
- **High quality paper**
- **Extra ink cartridge (if you're using an inkjet printer)**

Grab Your Best Friend and:

- **Your box of work samples or file of projects**
- **A computer and printer**
- **Your most recent résumé**

We can't stress enough the importance of having a friend help you with the assembly process. Friends can help you make wise choices for work samples, determine your management philosophy and goals, stuff paper into page protectors, make up tabs and exhibit cards, and help you through this somewhat frantic time. A good friend serves as a sounding board, and tends to ask questions of you that you wouldn't think of yourself.

Include These Sections in Your Portfolio:

- **Work Philosophy**
- **Career Goals**
- **Résumé**
- **Skill Areas—Determine different areas. Place work samples in appropriate areas**
- **Letters of recommendation (if available)**
- **List of professional membership and awards**
- **Community Service—Any work samples and letters available**
- **References**

Don't Forget to:

- **Create tabs for each section**
- **Make up work sample overview cards for your work samples on plain paper**

See Chapters 2 to 5 for specific guidelines for each of these sections.

3. Action Verbs

Action verbs are used in your résumé to indicate the types of actions you have done. Refer to Chapter 3, The Résumé, page 50, for more details.

Accomplished	Equipped	Organized
Achieved	Established	Paid
Adapted	Evaluated	Performed
Adjusted	Expanded	Persuaded
Administered	Expedited	Planned
Advanced	Filed	Presented
Analyzed	Furthered	Processed
Assessed	Gained	Produced
Assisted	Generated	Programmed
Authorized	Guided	Provided
Budgeted	Handled	Recommended
Built	Helped	Reduced
Chaired	Implemented	Repaired
Combine	Improved	Reported
Communicate	Increased	Researched
Completed	Initiated	Reviewed
Composed	Instructed	Revised
Conducted	Interviewed	Screened
Coordinated	Introduced	Served
Created	Learned	Set up
Delegated	Led	Simplified
Designed	Located	Strengthened
Developed	Maintained	Supervised
Directed	Managed	Supported
Displayed	Maximized	Taught
Edited	Modified	Trained
Employed	Motivated	Typed
Encouraged	Negotiated	Updated
Enhanced	Operated	Wrote
Enlarged	Ordered	

4. Department of Labor SCANS

Here is a list of baseline skills and competencies established by the Department of Labor known as SCANS. Use this skill list to review and organize your own skill sets or to assist in writing your skill descriptions for your résumé.

The Foundation—Competency Requirements:

Basic Skills	Thinking Skills	Personal Qualities
reading	thinking creatively	individual
writing	making decisions	responsibility
arithmetic	solving problems	self-esteem
mathematics	seeing things in the	sociability
speaking	mind's eye	self-management
listening	knowing how to learn	integrity
	reasoning	

Competencies—Effective Workers can Productively Use:

Resources	Interpersonal Skills	Information
allocating:	working on teams	acquiring and
time	teaching others	evaluating data
money	serving customers	organizing and
materials	leading	maintaining files
space	negotiating	interpreting and
staff	working well with	communicating
	people from culturally	using computers to
	diverse backgrounds	process information

Systems	Technology
understanding social,	selecting equipment
organizational, and	and tools
technological systems	applying technology to
monitoring and	specific tasks
correcting performance	maintaining and
designing or improving	troubleshooting
systems	technologies

From SCANS—Secretaries' Commission on Achieving Necessary Skills. 1991, U.S. Department of Labor

5. List of Templates on the Disk

The accompanying diskette contains files to help you save time while creating your career portfolio. Use these documents as a starting point. Customize these files and make them work for you. Feel free to change the fonts and rearrange information as needed. Each file was created in Microsoft Word 2000.

Faculty_Employer bios.doc - A contact list of people who are mentioned in your portfolio

Memberships.doc - A listing of your professional memberships

Recommendation request.doc - A sample letter for requesting a recommendation letter

References.doc - List your references and their contact information

Skillset.doc - A blank skill set serves as a starting point for creating checklists of your skills

Stmt of originality.doc - A basic statement indicating that the portfolio is your property and should be respected

SWOT Analysis.doc - A worksheet designed to help you plan your career

Work philosophy and goals.doc - List your work philosophy and career goals

Work sample overview cards.doc - Business card layout for printing overview cards used to identify work samples and materials in your portfolio

Index

portfolio (cont.)
  benefits 1, 2, 3–4, 17, 18
  contents 6, 19–20, 85–86
  defined 1
  electronic. See electronic
    portfolio
  equipment needed 9–10
  increasing salary & benefits 18
  job reviews 125–127
  leaving it overnight 122
  matching to the employer 118
  organizing 58–59
  planning 10–11, 33
  problems 16
  process 3, 17–18
  promotions 127–128
  proofing 92
  resistance to 16
  supplies needed 8–9
  updating 57
  using it 12, 117–128
printers 10
printing 144–145
professional development 15–16,
  79, 81
professional memberships 7, 36,
  79–80, 90, 151
promotion review
  using the portfolio 128

R
references 7, 12, 75–77, 151
  sample 76
  types of 75
résumés 6, 12, 90, 106, 117, 150,
  151
  action verbs 152
  basics 36
  chronological 37
  contents 35–37
  e-mailing 47
  example 44

faxing 48
focused 37
format 40
functional 37
gaps 39
government 38
key terms 45
keywords, using 42
length 40
new trends 45–46
online 45
performance 37
references 40
scannable 43–44
sending 46
tips 38
type style 40
types 37
websites 49
word choice 41

S
scannable résumés 43–44
  example 44
scanners 10, 143–144
SCANS, Dept. of Labor 153
service work samples 54
skill areas 6, 51, 151
  letters of recommendation 6
  skill sets 6
  work samples 6, 59
skill sets 6, 65–70, 90
  benefits 65
  creating 68–70
  customizing 69
  defined 65
  example of 66–67
  levels of ability 66, 68, 69
  on the job 70
  sample 66–67
  sources 66

CAREER PORTFOLIO VIDEOS

Career Portfolios are changing the way people interview by helping people plan, organize and document their work samples and skills. Using a portfolio can help you get a job, get a higher starting salary, show transferable skills, track personal development, and position you for advancement.

Now, two new videos are available to help you make the most of your portfolio. Each tape features advice and tips from the experts and takes a look at how real people use portfolios to advance their careers.

NOW AVAILABLE!

Creating Your Career Portfolio - Assembling Your Portfolio
This video overviews the career portfolio process and focuses on gathering supplies, work samples, and materials to include in a career portfolio. This video features interviews with professionals and students who have used the portfolio, tips from the experts, and detailed guidelines for putting together your own portfolio. 25 min. - $99.

Creating Your Career Portfolio - Using your Portfolio in Your Job Search
Once you have created your personalized career portfolio, how do you actually use it in an interview? This video features sample interviews and expert commentary to show the do's and don'ts of portfolio use in an interview setting. Learn tips on using the portfolio to your best advantage. 25 min. - $99.

Learn from the experts and authors! Get the set of two videos for $179.

TO ORDER:

Call 1/877-NAJORED (1-877-625-6733)
or fax your order to 1/877-NAJORFAX (1-877-625-6732)

Mail orders to:
NAJOR Educational Publishing

P.O .Box 36575
Indianapolis, IN 46038

Shipping:
$0-$99 - 7%
$100 and over - 6%
Indiana State Residents please
  add 5% sales tax

From Najor Educational Publishing, in partnership with Learnovation® LLC

3085